BEYOND THE WALL

Kim Austin is an active member of the House of Faith Ministries in Somerville, Tennessee and has been since 2013. Upon her arrival, we acknowledged her gift as a Prophetess, and she walks in that capacity. After pastoring her for over four years, we watched her grow in grace and knowledge of the Word of God.

This mighty woman of God is faithful. She is an intercessor and prays for the will of God for the people of God. This gifted speaker is also a dedicated jail ministry worker with compassion for the lost, including those incarcerated. She believes in having a servant's heart, so she serves by working the altar or whatever her hands find to do; she does it with all her might. Prophetess Austin loves the Lord and believes that what she has written is portentous for the body of Christ.

Sincerely,

Bishop Connie Wright

House of Faith Ministries
Somerville, Tennessee

I have known Kim and her family for approximately 40 years. There is nothing I would not do for her and her family. I have found her to be serious about her Christian walk. One day enroute to work we came upon a situation where drug addicts carried out some children from a fire grasping for breath. She did not hesitate; she knelt on her knees in the snow, and performed CPR. While serving the Detroit Police Department, she was firm and fair while discerning righteousness in her decision making. She was always compassionate with people in her community, seeking the greater good. An authentic, spiritual Woman of God, Kim has always had a thirst for hermeneutical matters and has respected the voice of pastors. She is a tribute to women in the ministry and a model for young women to look up to.

Dr. Pleze Gardner Jr., Ed. D.

Pastor of Christian Light M.B.C.
Detroit, Michigan

....

Thankfully, we have had the awesome privilege of serving in ministry with Prophetess Kim Austin. The seriousness of her God-given assignment has been a great inspiration to many. *Lest We Stumble* is a firm, yet passionate call to action that will impact the reader to reflect on the role the Church must take during these last days.

Pastor Lester and Evangelist Marine Payne

House of Faith Ministries #3
Alamo, Tennessee

FROM THE PASTOR'S DESK

To Prophetess Kim Austin: Great Speaker, Great Evangelist, and a Great Preacher, Woman of God. She loves and knows God, and is a loving and kind person who has fellowshipped down through the years. She has been a great inspiration to me and my church.

Pastor Jimmy Peete

El Bethel Non-Denominational Church

....

As an educator, Ms. Austin encouraged her other students and me not to give up and to finish what we start; she always found time to lift our spirits up and minister the Word of God.

Evangelist Patrina Thompson

El Bethel Non-Denominational Church
Memphis, Tennessee

....

Kim is passionate about her commitment to being a servant of Christ.

Helen Caldwell

Friend

LEST WE STUMBLE

Library of Congress Control Number: 2017934802

ISBN: 978-1-63308-274-8 (hardback)
       978-1-63308-261-8 (paperback)
       978-1-63308-262-5 (ebook)

Cover Design by *Velvet Long*
Interior Design by *R'tor John D. Maghuyop*

CHALFANT ECKERT
PUBLISHING

1028 S Bishop Avenue, Dept. 178
Rolla, MO 65401

Printed in United States of America

LEST WE STUMBLE

BY
KIM AUSTIN

CHALFANT ECKERT
PUBLISHING

FOREWORD

Why am I writing this book? Because shepherds are losing their flocks.

In 2005, I began hearing questions in my Spirit, questions relevant to church leadership and its operations. I also pondered on possible solutions to issues facing the church. The inspiration to write this book began in 2005, but my written format didn't start until 2012. I slept on it, conducted research through focus groups and surveys, and prayed about it for seven years. After careful consideration and consultation with the Holy Spirit, I began to write in 2012 and completed the manuscript copy December of 2016.

As a minister of the Gospel of Jesus Christ who has grown spiritually throughout my Christian experience, I want to share some thoughts on church leadership reorganization. By doing so, it is my hope that church leaders will consider why they do things the way they do, their operations, and consider avenues to retain their members. Perhaps we all will come away with a different perspective and rationale. I do not accuse church leaders of insensitivity or wrongdoing. Instead, I plead with them and give a wake-up call to reach out with God's love to those who need it most … lest they stumble. Many of my colleagues consider me qualified to address these important matters of the church, but God through His Holy Spirit has compelled me to write to church leaders and reveal why some people turn away from the church, and what we can do to turn them back to Christ.

Throughout church history, individuals, leaders, doctrines, policies, and practices have hurt some of God's children. Souls that could have been won to Christ and sealed with a heavenly destiny may have been lost because of the church's inability to create an atmosphere where the immature could grow. Many may have been hindered, mistreated, or shamed. Those who turned away because of their experiences with the local church may be in jeopardy of missing their God-given destiny.

History goes on, and it is still happening. Our leadership and practices may be the cause of our still hurting God's flock and possibly driving people away. As Christian leaders and ambassadors of God's Word, it is time to turn the tide and rethink our strategies to better care for our Christian brothers and sisters and bring new family members into God's Kingdom.

ACKNOWLEDGMENTS

Praise God from whom all blessings flow! My heart overflows with appreciation to God for His many blessings, among them insight to examine the inner workings of His Church, and for the wonderful husband, mother, family, and close friends He has given me.

The blessing of the LORD, it maketh rich,
and he addeth no sorrow with it.
Proverbs 10:22

I thank my husband John, who cares for me deeply as God's vessel, and who dedicates his life to Christ and Kingdom building. His quiet force steers the rudder of our marriage and home and has allowed me time at home to write this book.

I thank my mother who thinks I can do anything, my sons who wonder why I think I can do anything, and my close friends who encourage me to do anything.

I thank God for all the pastors and brothers and sisters in Christ who have been a part of my life, especially those who encouraged me to write this book. I thank every leader who has crossed my path because it is through each one of them that I have learned valuable life lessons.

DEDICATION

To my Mothers of Zion:

Aunt Frances Terrell,

Aunt Betty Howze,

and

Aunt Iown Smith.

TABLE OF CONTENTS

INTRODUCTION

STUMBLE:
To trip, to lose balance, to almost fall, or to make a blunder.

A hundred years ago, Christian principles were solid and defined. There was a clear distinction of between right and wrong, proper etiquette and Christian standards of living, all based on family values, biblical principles, precepts, statutes, and commandments. Most people went to church or made an occasional visit. Reverence for God's people, the local building, and the Word of God were respected by even those who admitted they were not living as Christians. Those who professed to be Christians made every attempt to conduct themselves as godly people. The local Church body consisted of strong families, bonded in love and by the blood of Christ. Traditions and spiritual values touched every community.

What happened? Fast forward to the twenty-first century, and we see the population is up, but church attendance is down, and some say it is at an all-time low. Yet against that backdrop, many church leaders are busy pursuing an increase in membership attendance to be able to maintain expenses of the local body and handle the costs associated with mega ministries, rather than focusing on equipping and increasing laborers to reach souls. Just as the Bible predicts, it appears the world (including the United States) is lost in ungodly behavior and character, religious practices. Godly traditions, for the most part, are being forsaken. Why do so many people have unresolved issues and why is God's wonderful creation (us!) turning so far away from Him? In an attempt to answer these questions, I present to you…

Lest We Stumble

PROBLEM STATEMENT

Wherefore the rather, brethren,
give diligence to make your calling and election sure:
for if ye do these things, ye shall never fall:
II Peter 1:10

Our world is in trouble. Drugs, war, violence, immorality, disregard for life, depravity, sexual promiscuity, and alternative lifestyles permeate society. These things and more hinder the moral fabric of our culture and move us ever more distant from God's plan for abundant life on earth. A Gallop International self-reported telephone poll conducted in 2013 showed that only 37% of people in the United States attended church weekly. In 2014, the Pew Research Center conducted the U.S. Religious Landscape Study and found that "the recent decrease in religious beliefs and behaviors is largely attributable to the 'Nones' – the growing of Americans, particularly in the Millennial generation, who say they do not belong to any organized faith." (Wormald, 2015).

It is not just the Millennials and the "Nones" who have become dependent on intellect, politics, mass media, and their five senses to steer their moral compasses. Even in the church, we find our definitions of family and commitment being redefined, and the line between right and wrong blurred to fit our lifestyles instead of God's Commandments, precepts, statutes, and principles. In some cases and places, the Church looks just like the world, and it has caused many to stumble. God's local body is no longer considered as light in a community of darkness nor a safe place from life's storms. We must revive our Christian standards, examine our behavior as godly leaders, and continue in the faith so that we do not cause others to lose their direction, and we will not be lost ourselves.

Lest they stumble.

CHAPTER 1

THE CHURCH ORGANIZATION

Not forsaking the assembling of ourselves together,
as the manner of some is; but exhorting one another: and so
much the more, as ye see the day approaching.
Hebrews 10:25

The Church and its operations are not the same as that of worldly organizations because the Church is a spiritual organism. What is the difference? Secular organizations make decisions based on human intellect, nepotism, and popularity. They select leaders based on human capabilities or a person's financial standing. Not so with the Church because a spiritual organism makes decisions that are envisioned and revealed through Prayer, the Holy Spirit, and communion with God who will make known those who should assist the pastor to lead the sheep. The Church must be careful not to let in spirits that would cause us to show favoritism.

Then Peter opened his mouth, and said, Of a truth I perceive
that God is no respecter of persons:
Acts 10:34

If you study leadership, a common theme emerges whether you are reading the expertise of John Maxwell, attending a leadership conference, or reading a leadership book. The theme is that to be a good leader, you must also be a good follower. In many instances, that is true, and if you are speaking from a natural or worldly perspective, then you may agree with this philosophy. The church has a different spiritual intent that is ordered by God to be a spiritual organism.

German sociologist and political scientist of the nineteenth and twentieth century, Max Weber, was a prolific writer on bureaucracy and management theory. According to Weber, for an organization to function effectively (whether a military structure, prison, government, or business), it must be formed with five elements:

1. Hierarchy of Authority. A Hierarchy of Authority must be established (levels of supervision and separation of staff from executives).
2. Rulification and Routinization. The organization must not only define the tasks to be performed, but must define the behavior of those belonging to the organization, and desired conduct of those involved with the organization (i.e. Code of Ethics).
3. Expertise. There must be a qualified knowledge base to guarantee proficiency. In some areas, a specialization is required.
4. Written Directives. There must be communication from and documented proof of receipt throughout the organization for clarity of instructions to ensure that those under authority know the standards, which also gives those responsible for tasks clarity of the organizational expectations, the method of acceptable performance (the standard or basic operating procedures, rules, and policies), and the delegation of authority to those who are responsible for getting the job done.
5. Division of Labor. Workers carry out the functions of the organization for maximum efficiency.

These five elements give members of an organization clarification and understanding of the mission and purpose, detailing how they will achieve its goals and objectives to ensure success.

In a natural organization (as compared to a spiritual organism), many problems occur which breed confusion and discontent such as inadequate communication and inequitable discretion (favoritism and nepotism) and misuse of authority and discretion when enforcing policies and procedures.

According to Weber, we must determine which tasks will be assigned to which group of people. These people must be given written and verbal directives to carry out the expectations of the organization. Therefore, the division of labor must also have clear lines of communication disseminated from the hierarchy.

Weber's theory can be applied to the Church, but when we look at these five elements from a spiritual perspective, we may see these elements through different eyes. The Church's mission statement is the Great Commission, assigned by Jesus Christ Himself.

> *Then Jesus came to them and said, "All authority in heaven and on earth has been given to me. Therefore go and make disciples of all nations, baptizing them in the name of the Father and of the Son and of the Holy Spirit, and teaching them to obey everything I have commanded you. And surely I am with you always, to the very end of the age."*
> Matthew 28:18-20

This Scripture clearly shows the function of the church and how it relates to the Body of Christ. The church's goals and objectives must be taught to the members of the spiritual organism so that God's work will be done in an orderly manner.

> *For God is not the author of confusion, but of peace, as in all churches of the Saints.*
> 1 Corinthians 14:33

In the Kingdom, for an organism to function effectively, it must be formed with the five elements applied in a different way:

1. Hierarchy of Authority. Believers must understand spiritual authority and that God Himself is at the top of the hierarchy with Jesus Christ as the cornerstone. Believers must profess Jesus

as their sovereign Savior and Lord, and accept the operation of the Holy Spirit in this earthly realm, acknowledging the Bible as the Word of God that contains the principles of holy living.

2. Rulification and Routinization - The Holy Scriptures make you wise, they are the rules of the Kingdom of God.

> *But seek ye first the kingdom of God, and his righteousness; and all these things shall be added unto you.*
> Matthew 6:33

3. Expertise. Ask God for wisdom and seek to know God intimately and what pleases Him. Through a strong belief system, we begin to develop a strong faith, enabling us to do the work and the will of Father God. Faith, praise, and worship please God.

4. Division of Labor. God wants us to worship Him, carry out the Great Commission, and be earthen vessels for the Holy Spirit's use. We are to labor for souls, consistently pray, and become disciple makers.

5. Written Rules. Spiritually speaking, the Bible is the ultimate written rule book. It contains the Commandments, His statutes, precepts, and promises. God's covenants with man, the Sacraments of Communion and Baptism, and God's laws for a Spirit-filled life are described within. Church policies that use the Bible as its base will create happy and productive members. However, many faith-based organizations may also follow the Apostle and Nicene Decrees, Faith Decrees, or the Church Covenant; they speak to the basic fundamental pattern of Christian conduct. Other ministries develop procedures and policies from the above mixtures.

These five elements assist us in understanding and carrying out the mission and purpose of the Church with clarity, successfully achieving its goals and objectives as we strive to accomplish the Great Commission. These duties must be taught to members of the local body. Otherwise, we become a non-functioning entity.

When a spiritual organism lacks any of the five elements, something important is missing, and the church will not be efficient or effective in carrying out the mission. The elements may seem to be an outdated, yet they contain fundamental principles of a well-functioning organization. Negative experiences or lack of direction in any organization may leave a person feeling victimized and alienated, whether a worldly or spiritual organization.

In the Church, the hierarchy does not change. God is at the head, and Jesus has all power in combination with God and the Holy Spirit to form the Holy Trinity.

Jesus saith unto him, I am the way, the truth, and the life: no man cometh unto the Father, but by me.
John 14:6

Then I will give you shepherds after my own heart, who will lead you with knowledge and understanding.
Jeremiah 3:15

The Word of God must be the absolute authority, but God has given us shepherds (pastors) over us as the spiritual authority of the local body.

Take heed therefore unto yourselves, and to all the flock, over the which the Holy Ghost hath made you overseers, to feed the church of God, which he hath purchased with his own blood.
Acts 20:28

As an organization, members conduct themselves in accordance with the Rulification that is in place to reach its mission. As an organism, Holy Spirit-led directions are given through the Word of God which are the inspirations of God on how those who assemble inside a body must conduct themselves, and are based upon rules developed from tradition, moral laws, Christian morals and ethics, as well as Godly principles lifting up a holy standard in an earthly place.

In a spiritual organism, our God is sovereign, and Jesus Christ is ever present through His Holy Spirit. Jesus left us the power and authority to do as He did and even greater things to save, heal, and deliver. The Holy Spirit is our guide, through His Word, His presence, and godly principles *Lest We Stumble*.

CHAPTER 2

WHY LEADERSHIP?

Let them alone: they be blind leaders of the blind.
And if the blind lead the blind, both shall fall into the ditch.
Matthew 15:14

**The Shepherd can cause the people to stumble and the people can cause the pastor to stumble.
Leadership is reciprocal.**
Kim Austin

What is leadership?

The ability to get things done through people to accomplish a common goal; the process of influencing activities of an individual or group toward a goal; influencing people to willingly strive for group objectives by exercising influence.

Why is there so much emphasis on leadership?

Wherever there is a group of people, whether large or small, difficulties often arise, especially when you attempt to get everyone to agree on any matter. Sometimes it is impossible, particularly in church organizations, unless the Holy Spirit is leading. We need the Holy Spirit to mediate interactions.

Everyone is not simply a follower; a few are leaders. Leaders are born naturally and spiritually. Managers learn how to manage people and use various forms of control. A supervisor's emphasis is on bossing others thus the term "boss." Managers and leaders have very different philosophies. Managers do what is best for the company, following corporate policy and procedures. Godly leaders hear the voice of God and serve God's people. Godly leaders follow the heart of God and their leader; they are guided by the Word of God and godly principles. Therefore, a good leader can draw people naturally and spiritually; people desire to assist the leader in whatever goal he is attempting to reach. There are many tools of leadership and the higher you go in the hierarchy, the more interpersonal skill may be necessary. Each echelon of leadership uses different tools or strategies to achieve the task at hand.

Why do we need a leader?

We don't want to go down the wrong path, and without a leader with good and proper vision, we will be the blind leading the blind. Without understanding and godly knowledge, we can't avoid dangers and snares. We need Holy Spirit-filled leaders who are willing vessels to be used of God and willing to follow as well as lead.

But we have this treasure in earthen vessels, that the excellency of the power may be of God, and not of us.
II Corinthians 4:7

On December 11, 2013, I heard a pastor speaking about leadership from the Book of Acts. When there is a mass of people, there are people issues and differences. In the book of Acts, there was a need to communicate and come to a consensus of understanding with the people. Fundamentals of communication include knowing how to agree to disagree and is often accomplished through a facilitator, a leader. Leaders often can settle differences. When people cannot communicate and negotiate their differences, contention and strife occur. Lack of communication or lack of understanding can be avoided when good leadership is present.

> *Come now, and let us reason together, saith the Lord...*
> Isaiah 1:18

He was speaking to His people concerning their rebelliousness and obedience. Today we, as God's people, should remember that disobedience leads to rebellious spirits and that the author of division and strife is always Satan. We must learn to identify his devices and listen to our leaders, and our leaders must listen to God, who hears the cry of His people.

Leadership Vision

People desire to follow leaders who seemingly know where they are going. Therefore, the leader's vision must be clearly articulated. People follow leadership that is genuine and caring, yet become suspicious when the vision seems to benefit only a select group or the pastor. The flock will scrutinize a pastor's agenda and projects to see if they are God-breathed or manmade. It comes with the territory. So, what does the leader's agenda look like?

- The best leaders are those who exhibit godly behavior before the people and in their daily lives, and are leaders who people know and trust, not to someone who is just trying to impress others on church days.
- Leaders should not attempt to entertain people, but their agendas should visually display that their vision is genuine.
- God's people must clearly see and buy into godly-focused and godly-ordained missions, which always yield success. If God is in it, the project will succeed.

David was a man after God's heart. God knew He could trust David to yield to the Holy Spirit and carry out God's vision.

> *And when he had removed him, he raised up unto them*
> *David to be their king; to whom also he gave their testimony,*
> *and said, I have found David the son of Jesse, a man after*
> *mine own heart, which shall fulfil all my will.*
> Acts 13:22

Just as God could depend on David, pastors must depend on their leaders to carry out God's vision for the local church. The congregation also needs to buy into the pastor's vision, believing that the vision is from God. When people don't believe that the vision is from God, they do not become stakeholders in completing the work needed to accomplish the vision. When members of the church follow the pastor and see him as a man on a mission from God, they must feel that they are a part of that mission and vision or they will not invest in its success.

Decisions are envisioned and revealed through prayer with the Holy Spirit and communion with God; He ordains those that should assist the pastor in His vision for the sheep.

We get more support from the congregation when an interest or idea is desirable to them. Perhaps then they will follow the leader out of love and not a sense of duty or obedience.

Leadership Effectiveness

What is *effective* leadership and what is *affective* leadership? Effective leadership gets the job done, but may be accomplished out of a sense of duty or religious practice. Affective, or emotionally-driven leadership, captures the joy of the task and comes from and is motivated by love. Jesus healed the sick, gave sight to the blind, and taught thousands when He delivered the Sermon on the Mount. He could have done these things out of a sense of duty, but I am certain He did them out of love. We can learn from His example.

In a spiritual organism filled with the Holy Spirit, our leaders will be anointed, living epistles exhibiting godly lifestyles. They will set godly examples. We must follow their lead so that people will see Jesus when they see us, and we can be accountable before God.

Holy Spirit-led leadership, is a combination of effective and affective leadership. Ordered steps by God can only be realized when we commune with God through prayer about how to lead His people. Communicating with God, on your knees in the corporate setting, lying prostrate before the Lord, standing in authority, and declaring and proclaiming His Word humbles the flesh and submits the physical body to the Holy Spirit.

Why Leaders Must Pray

Guidance and inspiration come from God, from the Holy Spirit, and from the Word. But communion is often strongest during prayer. Leaders should not only pray their individual morning and evening prayers but also lead their flocks in corporate prayer. Prayer is needed and required for every person leading every functioning entity of the local body. When you are in corporate prayer, you wholeheartedly have an anointed faithfulness, generosity, cheerfulness, and willing heart to lead your ministry with lovingkindness, aware of the process of disciple-making, and willing to be financially supportive and generous in your giving.

During prayer time, you are honoring God and allowing the Holy Spirit to speak to you, imparting knowledge, wisdom, and understanding to guide your ministry. You are also acting in a spirit of unity with the other ministries to strengthen the entire body. Corporate prayer is an absolute must! Through prayer, you can receive the anointing to minister to your flock, serve and teach others, and administer spiritual counsel on all matters that concern people. You must be filled with the Holy Spirit, who by the way, loves to commune with God the Father. We must ask ourselves: Is God first place in our lives, or are we acting out of a sense of duty and obligation rather than love for ministry?

Terms of Leadership

We have often seen the tenure of leaders extend beyond their divine purpose. This will also cause some leaders to begin to "lord" over people with manipulation, trying to control them and demand their obedience. That kind of leadership is outside God's divine purpose and is seen as strategic to effectuate planned responses. Jesus was Lord, but He did not "lord" His authority over others, instead exhibited love, caring, and servitude. Being a hard taskmaster over your flock robs people of their liberty in Christ Jesus and the desire to cooperate and participate in a Spirit of Unity. We have to be prayerfully careful about who we put in leadership. Through prayer and communing with God, He will give us revelation on who to select that will have the gifts and talents to lead, and the heart to lead well.

How you determine and evaluate skills is secondary to spending the time in prayer to hear from God about your choices. The Holy Spirit's still small voice will guide your choices.

Here is a helpful example of a spiritual organism's structure:

Leadership starts at the top and works in a well-defined hierarchal line of natural and spiritual authority. When the lines of order are broken, communication problems occur, and other nonproductive situations may arise.

Every situation is different, but here are some basic guidelines to consider:

- Leadership positions should change every year or two. This gives young, inexperienced gainsayers who have criticized the current leader the opportunity to get some experience and see how it feels to lead. Each new leader needs a mentor, someone who will help them over the hard spots and give them the wisdom of their experience so the new leader, lest they stumble.
- Remain a part of the ministry/auxiliary and help the new leader.
- Always express thankfulness by rewarding the members of the ministerial unit.

Prayer is the first essential element of successful leadership; the flock will follow because they exhibit a good example. They will realize that they are beneficiaries, it benefits them to follow! Once on board, they are Kingdom stakeholders, and they may become generous givers because they receive dividends. Leaders must commit to pray for their assignments, and so corporate prayer attendance is vital. Some leaders don't think meeting together for corporate prayer is necessary or required to hold leadership positions, just the payment of tithes and offerings. How can you assure that your manner of leadership is fruitful if you are not committed, loyal, truthful, and wholeheartedly willing promote God's righteousness? The Bible says not to forsake assembling together. Jews in the Old Testament fasted and prayed as a nation to gain God's favor and to repent of wrongdoing.

Change of leadership is healthy for the Body of Christ but should be spiritually led. In a spiritual organism, members feel like a family and not a "group of groups." Family members take ownership when they can contribute something to "the household." Some members of a ministry, or opponents of current leadership, remain obstinate and opinionated until they have to be the driving force. They can learn that healthy, spiritually-led change can cause the body to feel and operate like a family. They can learn what it is like to attempt to hold the family together while producing good fruit.

Follow the Leader

Leaders must be followers and servants. The Bible tells us that Jesus was the Good Shepherd, and a good shepherd herds and protects his flock and is, therefore, a good leader. You can get a sense of whether a leader is anointed and in the right calling by watching to see if he or she has followers willing to invest in the ministry of the leader and the vision. In contrast to an organization, managers and leaders are very different in philosophy. Managers do what is best for themselves and the company. Godly leaders hear the voice of God and serve God's people.

Leaders should first and foremost exhibit godly character, and be an example of the image and mind of Jesus Christ. They should also endeavor to mentor a protégé or two, perhaps the vice president or secretary of the serving ministry.

What happens when we don't mentor and help God's people grow in leadership?

It begins at the top with the associate ministers and the elders. Failure to mentor them may cause what is known as "Pulpit Wars." This is largely due to no direction or not using their gifts and talents. Much fruit has deteriorated in the pulpit perhaps because we don't know our calling, have not moved into our calling, or maybe just feel that the timing is not right and we are not developed enough yet. Many associates have left their pastors because of this; most did not want to leave, but wanted to progress in their divine purpose. The pastor should be aware of these issues and in some cases, just like an eagle pushes out the babies so they can learn to fly, push those who have potential out and let them spread their wings. Many associates become dependent upon the pastor and his work rather than learn and develop so they can help build the Kingdom. Some associate ministers even fall into the trap of modifying or changing the course of the pastor's vision. All must learn that the pastor is and has developed into what God called him to be. Now, what about you? Where is your fruit? Is it developing another branch, tree, or orchard? Or is it sitting trying to figure out whether it is an apple or applesauce? While it is wonderful to assist the pastor for a season, we must remember to develop our own fruit and assist him in the building of the Kingdom.

Sitting around can also cause spoilage, you can become envious and covetous of the pastor's vision and work. Fruit just sitting around spoils, draws insects, and gives off a foul odor. Of course, this does not apply to those who have a calling to assist the pastor in a particular area, such as aiding him in visitation, or in music or youth ministry. However, if we are not in our place, how can God bless us? Spiritual growth includes promotions and appointments from the pastor, inspired by God. Remember, promotion and exaltation come from God after your faithfulness to the Word of God has been proven.

Leader Qualifications

Leaders should be inspired to have the same Spirit as the pastor, who has prayed that person into the leadership role. Whether novices or seasoned leaders, they must be prayer warriors with the humbleness of heart to obey. Prayer is absolutely essential for the believer to increase faith, as are humility and obedience to the Word of God coupled with the willingness to receive instruction.

Leaders should be willing tithers and givers in offerings. Leaders should strive for growth to get to a higher level of maturity in the Word, increasing in faith, and becoming generous givers in every area of their lives. Leaders should be mindful of giving and serving in love as recorded in I Corinthians 13:13 and careful to not cause a stumbling block, as instructed in I Corinthians 8:9.

> *Every man according as he purposeth in his heart,*
> *so let him give; not grudgingly, or of necessity:*
> *for God loveth a cheerful giver.*
> II Corinthians 9:7

The more we fall in love with the Great Commission, the more we learn to give more than a tenth, give more than minimal service, and seek more of God, His presence, His wisdom and His sovereignty. After a while, we automatically respond to the needs of those in the Kingdom of God. Leaders who do not have these commitments may not be good choices for leadership.

If a leader is in the wrong place and leading in the wrong way, it can cause a shipwreck of sorts in God's house, a bad leader can cause the death or destruction of the entire congregation, just as a bad manager can cause a company to fall. In the Church, leaders can literally cause the demise of a new soul, never getting the opportunity to apologize, leaving the pastor (the Shepherd of the House) wondering what happened. Many times, souls were lost, and the pastor is totally unaware of the circumstances.

In Conclusion:

- Prayer is the first essential element of successful leadership.
- People follow good leaders because they set a good example.
- Spiritual leaders must be developed and develop others.
- Followers are beneficiaries. It benefits them to follow! They are stakeholders.
- Leaders and follows must be generous givers because they are stockholders who get to enjoy the dividends of God's blessings.
- They receive an earthly and heavenly reward. You cannot outgive God.

We must walk WORTHY of our calling in Christ Jesus:

W - Walking in Wisdom and always watching and praying
O - Obedience to the Word of God, always seeking God's plan
R - Reaching and seeking God's righteousness **First!**
T - Trusting in the Truth, and God's Word, to develop your Testimony of Triumph
H - Holiness, is the standard, the lifestyle
Y - Yielded to the Holy Spirit as our teacher, our guide, and con-victer to keep us in the narrow way, keeping us in confession and repentance...

Lest We Stumble.

CHAPTER 3

A GREAT FALLING AWAY

Even so it is not the will of your Father which is in heaven,
that one of these little ones should perish.
Matthew 18:14

In 2013, Pew Research Center brought together the leading experts in survey research on religion to discuss the rise of the religious "Nones" (religiously unaffiliated people, particularly Millennials including atheists and agnostics, who do not identify with any religion, and have little or no interest in religion, especially those denominations that try to dominate people's lives and actions), and other important trends in religion around the world (Liu, 2013). The United States Census does not collect information on religion. Gallup International, National Opinion Research Center (NORC), and Pew Research Center conduct research to provide the missing data. Pew Research is non-partisan and is not affiliated with any religion. They provide the raw data and statistical interpretation but leave it for the reader to draw their own conclusions.

Despite Millennial culture idealism, God desires that all might be saved. Generation X and Y have increasingly turned away from organized religion over the past decade. To maintain membership, we have seen changes in the operational standards of churches. Pastors and executive boards have sought ways to increase membership, community outreach for souls, and to cope with financial responsibilities. The moral decline in our society has caused some to make tradeoffs and compromises that appeal to Generation X and Y, many who no longer feel that Christian ethics or mores are necessary to guide their behavior. The generation of

"I-Feelers" and the "I-Thinkers" have enlarged influence that is steadily replacing the values set by the "Baby Boomer" generation. There are many driving forces causing the movement away from church attendance and religious ideology, and some wonder if the church as a foundational institution is still important.

What Do the Statisticians Say?

From March 28 to April 8, 2013, the following survey was done: The new, nationwide survey by the Pew Research Center's Forum on Religion & Public Life asked Americans whether having "more people who are not religious" is a good thing, a bad thing, or doesn't matter for American society. Many more say it is bad than good (48% versus 11%). But about four-in-ten (39%) say it does not make much difference. Even among adults who do not identify with any religion, only about a quarter (24%) say the trend is good, while nearly as many say it is bad (19%); a majority (55%) of the unaffiliated say it does not make much difference for society. (Liu, 2013, Jul 01, p. 1)

Scripture tells us that many will depart from the faith (I Timothy 4:1), that Christ's return is imminent (James 5:8), and that the lost are doomed to eternal damnation (Matthew 25:41). Many pastors have stopped preaching the existence of a hot hell for those who reject Jesus Christ, and many people think that hell is a philosophical allegory, not an actual destination in eternity. The revelation of who Jesus Christ is will come to pass.

Now we beseech you, brethren, by the coming of our Lord Jesus Christ, and by our gathering together unto him, That ye be not soon shaken in mind, or be troubled, neither by spirit, nor by word, nor by letter as from us, as that the day of Christ is at hand. Let no man deceive you by any means: for that day shall not come, except there come a falling away first, and that man of sin be revealed, the son of perdition;

II Thessalonians 2:1-3

Religion is important, but values, traditions, morals, and practices have changed over time, and people's expectations and preferences have changed as well. Although society benefits, it is rare to find those in today's culture who wholeheartedly observe biblical principles and the Commandments. Claude Fischer from the University of California – Berkeley while on the Pew Research Center's Religious Trends in the U. S. panel stated, "When Americans are disappointed in their churches, they exit and usually look for another church." (Liu, 2013, Aug 19).

When did our views change? When and why did we run astray of what our ancestors taught us? Is the decline related to new generations not embracing the values of previous generations? Could it be that liberal colleges and universities are changing the landscape of Christian values in our young people? There is little doubt that many influences work together to reduce the importance of religious beliefs and practices, not just in our young people, but throughout the life cycle. Another potential reason for decline for many conservatives is that organized religion as a whole has disappointed them in their churches, and many of them now opt to label themselves as "spiritual, but not religious" (Hout & Fischer, 2014).

If you do not attend church or involve yourself in any religious activities, how do you learn God's Word, or how to pray God's Word and where do you get Holy Spirit guidance to live a productive life? As a non-attender or a non-participant in a congregation, how do you know the behaviors that exemplify holiness and wholesome living?

> *How then shall they call on him in whom they have not believed? and how shall they believe in him of whom they have not heard? and how shall they hear without a preacher?*
> Romans 10:14

Social and Political Ramifications

Typically, religious identities drive politics, but now it seems the trend has reversed. Political and social ideologies seem to drive religious commitment. Michael Hout of New York University, reviewed data from

2002, stating that the "so-called greatest generation is passing away and being replaced by millennials who have much less attachment to organized religion and anything else, as near we can tell." (Liu, 2013, Aug 19).

Nones are on the increase, and the many causes span cultural, political, and generational shifts in society. Cultural components such as family and sexual values are reframing the emphasis (or lack thereof) of religious focus and practices. The Millennial generation is one of self-interest, self-reliance, and self-awareness, with little perceived need for God, salvation, or the Church.

If you were to ask some religious leaders what is spearheading this movement, the answer would be the flesh. One could readily see why the Bible speaks so much to the issues of the flesh. If we could eliminate the illegal needs to act outside the Bible dictates in the areas of sex, drugs, alcohol, tobacco, and other freedoms Millennials indulge in, it would be interesting to see if the Nones turned to the Church. Giving up the pleasures of the flesh may seem too difficult or not desirable and may be the root cause of people seeking to dictate their own actions free of scriptural guidance, even when those actions hurt them and cause guilt. Nones seem to operate on their sense of feeling what is right for them as individuals: politically, socially, sexually, and their ideas of family. Seemingly many of these issues are the root cause of people wanting to dictate their own beliefs away from the foundational Christian standards and precepts of living. A return to faith-based precepts of living would instill love, forgiveness, peace, and controlled behavior.

> *For all that is in the world, the lust of the flesh,*
> *and the lust of the eyes, and the pride of life,*
> *is not of the Father, but is of the world.*
> 1 John 2:16

Nones seem to operate based on feelings of what is right for them as individuals: politically, socially, sexually, and their ideas of family. People are crisis-orienting and often do not desire God until they are involved in tragedy. Some of their ideas are in direct conflict with Scripture and the church, and you would be in opposition to them if you were raised with strict values in these areas. Nones celebrate God their way. Many of those under thirty-five years old are busy with building their life desires, and God takes a back seat.

Set your affection on things above, not on things on the earth.
Colossians 3:2

Leaving God Behind for a Season

Children raised with Godly values often leave their root teaching to go out and explore the world and live in sin for a season, but later return to their Christian upbringing. The Bible says when they are *old*, they will not depart from it (doesn't say when they are young). In the interim, there is much to pray about whether our children get married and start raising a family, or stay single and remain committed to their careers. But as they get older, children turn back to God and again focus on the moral code and ethical principles they were raised with. As parents, it is hard to watch our progeny live in sin doing their own thing, only becoming conscious of God when tragedy occurs in their lives. Some may continue with their way of living as if there were no hell and no consequences, but when they turn about thirty years old, they come around and turn back to God. Perhaps these Nones look at their own children and want to give them an upbringing full of values and morals, so they clean up their act.

Train up a child in the way he should go: and when he is old, he will not depart from it.
Proverbs 22:6

This biblical principle, which may have had little or no effect on Nones prior to having children will impact them once they become parents. However, because they missed Sunday services, Christian fellowship, and the reading and acceptance of the Bible, a Christian lifestyle and a heavenly mindset will be foreign to them because they have forsaken the assembly with other believers in Jesus Christ. Participating in prayer services, observing the in-filling of the Holy Spirit and its impact on others in the local church may feel uncomfortable or seem ridiculous to them. In many cases, only the music will touch them emotionally on the few occasions they decide to attend.

> *Not forsaking the assembling of ourselves together, as the manner of some is; but exhorting one another: and so much the more, as ye see the day approaching.*
> Hebrews 10:25

If you can get a None to attend church and get comfortable, they will learn proper behavior, be uplifted spiritually, and develop friendships with their new Christian family that will affect not just them personally, but their children as well. The practice of attending for emotional purposes and to be entertained will now shift as they are now developing lives of others.

Finally, the falling away from Christianity, loving God, and regular attendance at church, is not a good thing, and the growth of Nones has impacted society negatively, which causes a departure from godly standards. Findings from the author's surveys revealed a lack of belief in the "spiritual" realm and an attitude that as long as they attend services, they felt good about themselves. However, this attitude does not cause them to "live" the Word of God. As a result, there is no regenerative change, no repentance, and no conversion occurring in the local body.

Although the Pew Research Center published findings that eighty-seven percent of Nones were not looking for a religion (Liu, 2012), it should be noted that the Church is alive and well, and Jesus Christ leads and presides through the Holy Spirit as a spiritual organism, as opposed to the local organized religion, which may not thrive.

Why is there a discussion about the decreasing numbers of church attendees? Why is the local church body so important in a society of violence, disrespect for authority and life itself? In a society where moral values have declined, why do we need the Church? The twenty-first century includes three or four generations, and some of the later generations have not been taught family and godly parenting based on biblical principles that previously had been passed down from generation to generation.

Early Years

Children have been and continue to be carted off to daycare, while mothers spend ten hours daily working to sustain their family. Children become socialized in day care centers or with a babysitter, and some have grown up on their own without solid parental bonding. The home and church are the primary institutions that teach family values, ethics, and beliefs. Many individuals have grown up in the selfish society of "It's all about me," and "if it feels good, it is good." We have a generation of individuals who feel others should not only support them but are responsible for their total well-being; a generation of people who have a sense of entitlement. When character, values, love for others, and similar instruction are not taught in the home, there is little incentive or desire to go to church, and sometimes no knowledge of the benefits of living a godly life. Values based on God's existence and the promise of eternal life, are nonexistent, and many do not know the requirements of getting to heaven. Could this be why there is so much moral depravity, violence, lack of respect for authority, and lack of caring? Why hope is diminishing for many in our society? Why we don't think that attending church is important?

Midlife

From 35 to 50 years, we are rearing families then we revert to traditional ideas to perhaps keep our children from going astray, or we simply have an attitude that we have "been there, done that" and discover it was not all that exciting anyway. That is if we make it out unhurt and undistorted. During childrearing, we tend to go back to our roots of Christianity. We return to Christian ethics and principles, statutes, judgments, and moral code because we know it worked, and it makes sense again. We can now apply the Word of God to our lives in practice and learn to develop a love for God. For the most part, we can now become living epistles.

As pastor, leaders, neighbors, authoritative figures, educators, we are responsible for living out an example before men and women. We accountable to God if we compromise His standard to try new ways of doing things in an attempt to bring change or a more desirable effect.

Over 50

As we get older and have experienced life, religion becomes more important than at any other time in our lives. We have learned the dangers of following youthful lusts and now pray for our families who are adamant about living their own lives. Once we cross that fiftieth decade, the pride of life diminishes, and we find that we need for someone to love us, we desire extended companionships, and often we turn to the Church. Exceptions occur, however, and some of those who are part of the lost generations (Generations X and Y) that were not taught values, principles, and standards continue to keep doing things their way, the way that has seen right in their own eyes; their way has always worked for them contrary to biblical principle.

> *Do not be wise in your own eyes; fear the Lord and shun evil.*
> Proverbs 3:7 NIV

For those, it may take tragedy, death, or terminal illness to get them to reach for God.

Some Statistics from Pew Research Center:

1. While those with no religious affiliation are less negative than other U.S. adults in their assessment of this trend, only about a quarter of the religiously unaffiliated (24%), say it is a good thing that more people are not religious. About as many (19%) say it

is a bad thing, and a 55% majority says it does not make much difference for society.

2. Americans who attend religious services regularly are particularly likely to say that the growing number of people who are not religious is a bad thing for society. About seven in ten (69%) people who attend worship services at least once a week say this trend is a bad thing, compared with about a third (35%) of those who attend services less often who say the same.

3. The difference between weekly attenders and those who attend less often holds across nearly all major religious groups, including white evangelical Protestants, white mainline Protestants, black Protestants and white non-Hispanic Catholics. But there is no statistically significant difference in views on this question between Hispanic Catholics who attend Mass at least once a week and those who attend less often. (Liu, 2012).

Over 60

When we reach 60 and beyond, we finally figure it out and see through the church politics, changes, and disengagement. If we are no longer able to stand in positions, sing in the senior choir, or serve on the mother's board, it may seem as if there is no room for us as the elderly except for an occasional mention on Seniors Day. We often conclude as we enter assisted living and nursing home care, that no one really cares about all the contributions we made and all the works we did in the past. We begin to feel unimportant and not needed, and some of us become Nones, unaffiliated with anyone. If the older membership has been replaced by younger members, we may even be denied funeral services if we are not continually tithing our monies, which may be controlled by other family members. Many families or individuals who have not been on the church roll for years past have not contributed tithes and offerings, or who have not worked hard with programming have experienced this disconnect. Unfortunately, some churches define membership by who has been active at church and contributed tithes in the last 90 days.

CHAPTER 4

APPOINTED LEADERSHIP

Who is Really Running Things?

Although these next few chapters are sensitive, we need to talk about them. I make no accusation, but want to provoke thought for people who hold positions in local assemblies. Many souls have been lost because of a spirit known as "Respecter of Persons." When you show favoritism, you allow the "Respecter of Persons" spirit to influence your decision making, and you can expect two things: incompatible goals and different classes of people receiving differential treatment.

Individuals enter the local assembly and begin the journey of seeking a walk with Jesus, or maybe they have been drawn for other reasons. They have professed Jesus Christ as Lord, and they're learning how to be possessed by Christ in their inner being. As they grow, they get involved in ministries. Perhaps they join the choir, but only certain people are allowed to lead. They are on time but notice that others don't have to be. It becomes obvious that the rules only apply to some of the people, and that others are given preferential treatment. They quickly find out who is running things, and often it is either the First Family or the Founding Family that the newcomer is looking at. Even if those with status did not ask to be role models, they still are.

Newcomers have no way of knowing that those first members were the ones who gave, did, organized, and sacrificed to build the local church body when no one else was there. They became the original leaders because they had to. As time went on, these initial leaders became mentors as the congregation grew. They didn't stop but grew and mentored others, so they earned their rightful place as leaders in the local congregation, which is as it should be. God's gifting is reciprocal: As you give to others, He increases you and thus is the blessing of service.

Why is this important? Because if a member of the first family or founding family does not favor you and there is a disagreement, other family members may side against you and side with their family member. Unfortunately, first families and founding families often clash and cause major schisms in the local body. You may be accepted by the first family and even develop a very close relationship, but failure to agree with them too many times will cause hurt feelings and may cause you to leave the church. A similar situation occurs when you don't stand with the founding family or other politically strong group in the church who has influence over most of the congregation. It would be nice if we had more relationship-building going on in a spirit of unity instead of politics in a spirit of favoritism.

When one person is the target of several issues of disagreement, he or she may be accused of interfering with the elites' anointing or going against the pastor's wishes. When that happens, the person under fire will lose their place in the ministry, be accused of "touching God's anointed," and be accused of going against the pastor's wishes. Some will become discouraged and may even stop believing in God's love, the Word of God, and the spokesperson of God, becoming totally turned off to the local church body. That person may be turned off and turned away from the things of God because God's people caused hurt. It would take nothing less than the Holy Spirit-led organism to heal the situation and get the person back into the sheepfold and shelter of God's love and protection. He or she may or may not be rooted and grounded in love with God and His Word, yet it can happen in either case. Therefore, we should not look at the messenger, but always get the message of love. Prayer for lost individuals must be sought by the "praying wall;" our agenda must always be the same as God's agenda, winning lost souls to Christ. Lest we, the very elect be lost.

For the Son of man is come to save that which was lost.
Matthew 18:11

First and Founding Family Control

One of the most fragile relationships in the church is with the pastor and the first family. This is particularly fragile because of the female ratio of the church today. Many don't believe in the position of co-pastor, which is usually held by the male pastor's wife. This is important because many stumblings have occurred when leadership has ended up in bad situations because of an unfortunate experience with the Jezebel Spirit. This treacherous spirit seems to be prevalent in every local assembly. When that spirit is present, the people influenced by it will constantly sow seeds of discord, criticizes others, always tries to get the upper hand, refuses to admit wrongdoing, and takes credit for everything (30 Traits of the Jezebel Spirit, 2016). The wife as co-pastor keeps this spirit in check because the wife can assist in the necessary counseling sessions and teachings of that local assembly which may contain a large percentage of women, children, and young people. The Church Mother can also assist the First Lady with delicate situations better handled by female leaders in the church instead of the pastor. Most female issues should be handled by the female leaders; It is a well-known fact that Satan loves discord and causes conflict between female relationships; mothers may have intense relationships with their teenage daughters, female leaders in the Church, as well as women supervisors in an organization, often have difficulty with female employees. Therefore, Christian counseling by mature female leadership may often be the best way to handle these types of matters.

Women in the church sometimes compete for the pastor's attention, and the Jezebel spirit has an opening to take control by planting thoughts such as "I can do it better than you," and "I want to be in control," and "only I can serve the pastor." Remember the purpose of the Jezebel spirit is to separate, divide, and cause contention and strife; this spirit's motives are to create jealousy and take control. All Jezebel wants is attention! Her attack is often steered in the direction of unmarried women or women whose fathers abandoned them.

As pastors, how do you fight the Jezebel spirit? Praying for discernment and awareness is great spiritual armor, as well as equipping leaders through training.

Deacons and Tithers

Other controlling spirits lie with those individuals who believe that the local assembly cannot thrive without them. This is often prevalent with members who are generous with tithes and offerings. They like to shine for the pastor's anniversary. They may try to control church activities and projects, thinking that if they do not, the project will not get done correctly. Pastors must be wise and alert to avoid letting these spirits take over their board and church leadership.

Chairpersons

Select people with the most experience in all areas when possible, but also remember to give those with less experience the opportunity to serve and grow in leadership under the mentoring of the most experienced. God does not call the qualified; He qualifies the called.

Ministerial Units of the Local Body

Pastors and ministerial leaders must pray for individuals in their ministries, but also pray for the protectors and birthers (the Mothers), and ask God to give the chosen special anointing to succeed. Otherwise, these individuals will not be spiritually supported; unable to discern and hear the Holy Spirit relative to the anointed assignments, revealing those who will be helpful in that area of ministry.

Counseling and prayer resolve issues that may come up in the unit or auxiliary. How do we deal with difficult people? We accomplish this through excellent interpersonal skills and spiritual guidance. Leading a particular ministry is designed to help the pastor and other units or auxiliaries of the church. Those ministries do not exist so the leaders can create their own "little kingdoms." Leaders need to care for those under them so as not to hurt or hinder their spiritual growth. New members want to feel a part of their new church family, and leaders must take

extra care not to alienate them, put them down, or cause them to feel that they have no valuable contribution. Leaders must embrace and get to know their protégés and love them as newborn babes in the family of Christ. Good leaders will identify and seek out their God-given talents and abilities, and work with and mentor them so that they become grounded in faith, service, and fellowship. An early departure may cause their roots to be broken or to wither away.

Watch out for attacks of self-righteousness. Seasoned members sometimes get uppity and lose God's righteousness. Instead of lovingkindness, self-righteous leaders cause others to depart. Has anyone ever left the Church or a unit because of YOU? I beseech you, if they are still around, ask God for guidance in healing the matter, then humbly ask that person to forgive you and allow you to amend the situation. Leaders must be humble and obedient to God's Word. When confronted with conflicting views regarding worldly ways or God's Way, we should be in careful submission to the Holy Spirit and obey His lead. Peter, when addressing the Sanhedrin spoke this:

> ***Then Peter and the other apostles answered and said,***
> ***We ought to obey God rather than men.***
> Acts 5:29

Fellowship and Followship

Some proclaim "follow-ship" to be first and fundamental when speaking of leadership, but perhaps fellow-ship is more important because emphasis is placed on sharing, communicating, and understanding. Fellowship replaces hypocrisy and manipulation so that newcomers see, feel, and hear consistent messages from church leadership. Remember initially, outsiders are more confident in their five senses before they learn to be led by the Holy Spirit. Leaders must be saturated in the anointed oil from God, there is no room for natural senses, but the Holy Spirit must be the guide.

Obedience requires a great understanding of God's heart. I previously was of a mindset that I should obey everything church leaders told me. I have since learned to pray and seek God's guidance because I felt that everyone wanted to tell me what to do. "Leader Wannabees" control freaks, glory seekers, false prophets, and pastors "who went and were not sent." Unfortunately, there are pastors who are lovers of themselves are out there, and they give God and His people a bad name. WOW, no wonder people are confused! The mature Saints of God must be careful and spiritually discerning. When they are not, people do some strange things. How else could people like Jim Jones or cults get people to do ridiculous, even fatal acts in the name of obedience? Sometimes we don't understand, but our spiritual antennas must go up when something is tried by the Spirit and not met with spiritual understanding. In those times, pray and fast; ask God to give you clarity.

CHAPTER 5

WHY THIS CHURCH?

Not forsaking the assembling of ourselves together, as the manner of some is; but exhorting one another: and so much the more, as ye see the day approaching.
Hebrews 10:25

God is greatly to be feared in the assembly of the saints, and to be had in reverence of all them that are about him.
Psalm 89:7

What are you looking for in a church?

What are the characteristics that people desire in a church setting? Have individuals examined their preferences? Do you ask yourself whether you are comfortable in a large or small ministry? Is it a family preference? Do we attend a church that is in close proximity to our homes? Is the church the center of our social lives? Are we really seeking a church to get to know God or do we just attend what is convenient and comfortable? Do we attend a church that has a service for one hour, giving us the ability to then be off to enjoy the rest of our day? What is it we are really looking for?

Do we want to participate in the activities of the church? Is the church serious about addressing the needs of the community? Do we desire the work of ministry or are we attracted to fads, entertainment, and other trends of the twenty-first century? Do we attend because there is a charismatic speaker? The main question we need to ask ourselves is whether this local assembly motivates us to "live" the Word of God and commit to the Great Commission, as delineated in the Matthew chapter 25 as a constant reminder of who we are and what we should be doing.

As believers, it should be a habit to attend church with a desire to worship and hear the Word of God. We need to hear sermons that warn us of sinful behavior, educate and feed our spirit, urge us to commit to righteousness, encourage us during times of testing, and allow us to experience the power of the Holy Spirit to indwell us and His sanctuary.

Nonetheless, there are some sensitive issues we need to talk about, because Nones and others who have left the church, talk and think about these issues in their private settings. We are hopeful that every leader in the local assembly is concerned with saving souls. It is unfortunate the purpose is overshadowed at times with programming and improper motives.

Regeneration and Conversion

First and foremost, we must be prepared to minister to the community. That is why we must attend a local body that equips us to meet the needs of individuals in the community as well as those in the local body. Have you ever selected a house of worship with the hope that you will see change in your life? Perhaps a friend has been changed from what they used to be, and so you have hopes that attending will help you change your behavior. Perhaps the last thing we look for is a local assembly with a pastor that focuses on behavior change and regeneration and conversion of the old man into a new man in Christ Jesus. We must ask ourselves why the same people are sitting in theses churches on Sundays and Wednesdays of every week, but not experiencing the converting and regenerating change that will enable them to go make disciples. How can they have a heart for witnessing when there is no willingness in their spirits? Has the willingness to say, "yes" to God been birthed out of them? These are questions that many pastoral and leaders have asked themselves. How do we correct flawed thinking and can we correct it?

Let's look at our motives for attending a particular church. Do we want to participate in the activities of the church? Is the church serious about addressing these needs? Do we desire the work or do we attend because we have a dynamic speaker? The question we need to ask ourselves is whether we are motivated to live the Word of God and are we motivated to commit to community service? We should keep the 25th Chapter of Matthew as a constant reminder of who we are and what we should be doing.

Unfortunately, sometimes people, government, and the community question large endeavors such as teen and daycare centers, and they often suspect that they are personal endeavors rather than meeting the need for the congregation or community. When the entire congregation, both young and old, are not shareholders of the project, they will not have confidence in the work of the local church. The congregation must know that their finances and efforts are committed to helping others. Jesus answered His disciples when they asked Him about meeting the needs of others, and He gives us emphatic direction. For those who carried out His Word, He separated to the right. For those who did not do the work, those on His left, He said, "Depart from me…" because His work had not been performed.

For I was an hungered, and ye gave me no meat:
I was thirsty, and ye gave me no drink. I was a stranger,
and ye took me not in; naked, and ye clothed me not;
sick and in prison, and ye visited me not.
Matthew 25:42, 43

Then shall he answer them, saying, Verily, I say unto you,
Inasmuch as ye did it not to one of the least of these,
ye did it not to me.
Matthew 25:45

And these shall go away into everlasting punishment:
but the righteous into life eternal.
Matthew 25:46

Meeting Needs

How do we address the needs of the community when we ourselves are not compassionate about the needs of others but only have a zeal for our own selfish interests? What are some of the needs that we can assist with in the community of God's people?

Most individuals agree that we need a sense of unity and belonging, which generally comes from the family unit. Where are American families today? I think we will agree that the strength of the family unit has been broken down because of the absence of our basic moral fabric and commitments to each other. We lack commitment to the institution of marriage, to parenting children, to the neighborhood, and to the work ethic (and the list may go on).

We know we need day care centers structured in such a manner as to modify the behavior of our children and Christian staff workers who instill strong moral values and principles in children (attributes such as character, trust, integrity, truth, giving, sharing, and love). Christian ethics should be coupled with behavior modification and support classes for the parents.

Employer commitments to work with faith-based organizations, such as employee assistance programs, can yield effective intervention strategies into the lives of those in the Church. These programs can be developed and manned by Holy Spirit-filled leaders. The Church should endeavor to create and manage these types of projects that address prevalent community and family problems such as homelessness of adults and youth. This is not just an endeavor for the Catholic Church, who have impacted the community by feeding the poor and destitute for many years. It is time for other denominations and faith-based organizations to get involved, those who propose to be Christians. Coalitions with family members and social agencies can alleviate many community problems, especially the treatment and housing the mentally ill. There are so many problematic areas where the spiritually-minded church can be effective in meeting the needs of people. After all, healthy, sober-minded people make good families, and families make up healthy churches.

Next, let's examine our current activities. Most churches seem to be focused on addressing the youth. We don't want to lose them to activities such as gangs, drugs, sex, and other negative impact factors, so addressing their need to belong is a priority. However, are these activities designed to save our youth or entertain our youth? Are they balanced to include all members of the church, or are we just youth oriented? It is great to include youth programming because youth are the church of tomorrow; but will it be a spiritual church of tomorrow if we do not assure that they are filled with the Holy Spirit? We must be careful that youth programming does not overemphasize worldly trends. Will our youth be empowered to handle the pressures of life and stand on the promises of our God or will they be overtaken by other gods? Will they be seeking the things of the world or God's Kingdom? Let's consider our priorities, what is it that we really strive for? The local body needs to address both natural and spiritual needs of our youth to ensure strong spiritual development.

The revelation of Jesus speaking is still profound! The thought makes you shudder. The Mission of the Church should mimic the Great Commission; Christ makes it very clear relative to the priority of the Church and those who lead the Church.

The Church has to go beyond our beautiful and comfortable edifices, which in some cases, costs millions of dollars. Should we continue putting that kind of money in buildings or should we be building in the hearts of men?

Is it possible that we have lost the will to commit to Christ's vision of seeking the lost? The revelation of Jesus speaking to the issue of the lost is profound! It should make us shudder! Christ makes it very clear that saving the lost is the priority of the Church and those who lead the Church.

Are we satisfied with just attending services to feel good about ourselves? That we have done our duty when we go to church? Have a wonderful praise and worship experience? Then go home as if we have no commitment to the work of Christ? As though there are no worldly problems? It is possible that we have lost the vision of Christ and lost the will to commit to the Great Commission because we are not seeking the lost.

Finally, we need to ask ourselves whether we are being spiritually and naturally prepared to serve others. Are we willing and equipped to take on the task and issues of the needy? Are we preparing our youth with the resources to be successful? We need to have an urgent cry for our youth who have gone out into the world. We don't want to go into judgment without the fruit from our lives.

Small, Medium or Large Churches

Regardless of the size, it is important to determine your personal preferences and how you will accomplish your spiritual development. Individuals should not attend an assembly where the Word of God is not being taught. The Word of God should change your life and worldly behaviors associated with it. Therefore, being honest and understanding your needs require a careful and truthful examination of you and your family's needs. Loving God and loving God's people should become your priority. If you change local assemblies, let it be for spiritual growth, and by all means, be guided by the Holy Spirit. The Holy Spirit will guide you to speak with your pastor and make your departure a peaceable change with no hindrances.

Sometimes there are various reasons you prefer a ministry. It should be chosen not on size or popularity but on the growth and love of God being performed in you. When you choose properly and are led spiritually, you will not have any problems with support, obedience, and growth in that ministry.

The Megachurch

When we ask God to enlarge our tent, what are we really asking? Are we making an attempt to grow the church or are we allowing God to add to the Church? Are we enlarging a building or are we enlarging our ministry? When we attempt to grow the church in our own power seeking large membership rolls, we struggle with all the pitfalls that the journey brings. But when God adds to the church, all obstacles are removed, and there are no financial burdens or stumbling blocks.

What about the *Megachurch*? Why do we build them? Do we count up the cost? Leaders generally ask the congregation if they're really willing to endeavor upon these huge projects. It can be quite a financial responsibility, as well as a tedious journey that demands financial commitment by the local assembly leaders. I'd like to examine at least two perspectives.

First, we must remember that Megachurches can be a maze for newcomers and so Megachurches are not for everyone. We must remember that some individuals prefer to be personally involved with their pastor and the congregation. Relationships are important to them, this type of "up close and personal relationship" may often be absent in the Mega organization. Generally, the Megachurch has "Mini Ministries" within the Megachurch, which serve the needs of their people relative to a specific area. That is good from an impersonal perspective; some individuals do not feel the need to know everyone in the congregation.

Bank loans are often contingent upon proving that a church has a certain number of bonafide regular-attending, dues-paying members. It may be a qualification for some banks; proof that the assembly has membership stability. Many banking organizations have loaned monies to a church and the next thing you know, the church doors are closed, and the flock doesn't know why; then they find out that the church has defaulted on the loan. Horrifying stories have been heard too many times and cause individuals to leave an assembly; the members' natural experience tainted before they became rooted and grounded in knowledge and understanding about their spiritual experience of conversion and regeneration.

Support

The financial commitments to the operations of such a large endeavor must come from not just the pastor, but the people who have agreed to the financial responsibility. There are more bills and more service commitments when we chose to enlarge the church, and a need for more workers to serve people. In many cases, the Old Testament obligation of ten percent just won't meet the financial demands. Pastors will need to preach and teach about generous, even sacrificial giving. The local congregation must desire to meet the needs of Kingdom building through laboring in prayer and service, not just having a mind to be individually blessed with materialism. It takes work!

> *Every man according as he purposeth in his heart,*
> *so let him give; not grudgingly, or of necessity;*
> *for God loveth a cheerful giver.*
> II Corinthians 9:7

The Word of God further tells us of the principles of sowing and reaping. Another Scripture tells us in the Gospel of counting up the cost.

> *For which of you, intending to build a tower,*
> *sitteth not down first, and counteth the cost,*
> *whether he have sufficient to finish it?*
> Luke 14:28

If the move is of God, then the church will spiritually grow as the souls prosper, and the people will not feel hardship or become jealous of the growth.

Building a new edifice may be a real need designed to address problems of people in the community. There are many societal problems in the community that only the resources of a Mega Church can meet, so some churches have become Mega Ministries to meet those needs. The pastor and the outreach workers must meet people where they are and love them by helping them in their situations. This may require a need for the several classes ranging from parenting classes to behavior modification classes. The building of schools, daycare facilities, soup kitchens, and shelters for the homeless are worthy causes for the Church. When these needs are met for the purpose of drawing souls and assisting the community, then we know the Great Commission is being fulfilled, and God blesses these endeavors.

Then there are some churches that have strained resources and are attempting to meet natural needs. They may give to the community during Thanksgiving and Christmas. However, having said this, we have seen many churches desperate to meet the financial needs with strategies of filtering finances through other resources such as partnerships and corporations, via grants and donations. An organization desiring to facilitate ongoing programs such as youth and daycare centers may need to develop a separate organization, claiming nonprofit status. The separation of church and state will bring about different financial requirements that conflict with a local assembly's goals.

Some churches may not be familiar with obtaining and administering grants; most think they have a lot of latitude in programming and financial responsibilities. They may think it is okay to use the finances themselves by making line budget changes. Upon receipt of these funds, regardless of the amount, their first order of business was a budget line item change in an attempt to gain control over the funds. Most don't realize that you must not only manage, secure, and write a grant, but you must be accountable for the administration and quarterly reporting of those funds. Let us not forget the fiduciary responsibility.

For years local assemblies sought to be recipients of government monies by developing programs for grant funding monies, only to discover that the church and state relationship may need to be separate; God's way of taking care of His people is to be self-sustaining. Many reports have shown up on the news about church secretaries and others being indicted for malfeasance of government funds. The purpose of the grants is only to receive temporary funding until you can obtain sustainability from the benefactors of that community.

Many of these programs were great programs that were developed to really benefit the needs of the community, but the failure to acquire continuous sustainability caused the programs to fizzle out due to lack of funding. Therefore, the beginning of a good work fails individuals and the community causing us to stumble because we did not count the financial and personal costs involved.

Are You Here or There or Everywhere?

There are some congregations that have grown so large that is it quite common for pastors to have more than one location. In some local assemblies, the pastor has become a "Traveling Shepherd" who must depend on other leaders to maintain the ministry. In the past, unless you were a Bishop or evangelist, you rarely saw this phenomenon. Is this possibly a characteristic of the Megachurch? Pastors would only leave their flock for a good reason. Of course, what comes along with the growth is the acceptance of a congregation who is mature enough to be advised and taught by the pastor's associates or ministerial staff. However, for an assembly, particularly with a large percentage of new babes in Christ, being away on a regular basis may not be a good decision.

When the Pastor is away, who has he left in charge? If the necessity of travel to a second or third service is unavoidable, then is there a greater level of accountability and assurance that the spirit of the person left in charge has the same spirit as the pastor's spirit? If not, are you leaving yourself open for a breach in the spirit of your assembly?

Secondly, is the Holy Spirit deliverance power dwelling in the assembly without God's anointed and appointed leader? This is why pastors must "pray in" their leaders. It is of great importance that his prayers to God concerning these engagements or responsibilities are in agreement with God. Many times, commitment to these types of engagements can be out of a sense of loyalty to other pastors; then there are other times when they can be healthy fellowship for growth. The Holy Spirit will speak in agreement with His choice so that the needs of His sheep are being met. Frequent absences of shepherd and leaders and even congregational members may be dangerous. It is, however, acceptable for fellowship with other churches, conferences, and training, for the purpose of growth; but regular attendance away from the ministry should carefully be considered.

Since the Church is now in perilous times, most congregations are in need of watchful eyes and constant prayer, because of the ravenous wolves. The enemy is constantly looking to devour "Kingdom Builders" and will stray a sheep away when left unattended.

Feed the flock of God which is among you,
taking oversight thereof, not by constraint, but willingly,
not for filthy lucre, but of a ready mind
I Peter 5:2

Has God given us members and offices to perfect the Saints? We are ligaments fitly joined together, to supply every joint for the building of the local body, right? So why does one pastor have to go everywhere? Is there no man of God that God has placed in that area? Usually, we find that, unless ordained by God, the pastor will soon burn out, he will become tired and unsettled. Time with family and the congregation may be lost because there are only so many hours in a day.

Again, these are issues that non-church attenders are questioning, practices that cause others to question the validity of the Church. As leaders, we need to be aware of the tactics the enemy uses, in the minds of individuals who have left the Church, or address the minds of these Nones (non-attenders) who are in jeopardy of stumbling and straying away.

CHAPTER 6

MONEY, GIVING, FAVOR, AND WEALTH

For wisdom is a defense, and money is a defense:
but the excellency of knowledge is, that wisdom
giveth life to them that have it.
Ecclesiastes 7:12

The Storehouse

The principle of a "full storehouse" is through obedience to tithing and giving of offerings; even for the Church. The spiritual growth of mature believers will be manifested when the congregation becomes generous givers in accordance with the Scriptures. God forbid that He allows the continuance of His church, dependent upon the "minds of people." If the storehouse is not financially sound, it is because the people do not obey the Scriptures and or the congregation is not walking in faith.

So how does the church gain wealth? What does God say about it? Does the church tithe back into the community? Is the local body itself operating by faith? In many churches, only 25 or 30 percent of the congregation are actually committed givers. So, where do we get the finances when we have overextended ourselves with expensive mortgages, taxes, and utilities?

These types of situations are why leaders must be prayed into positions of trust and responsibility. They must be responsible and accountable to God and the local body, and flexible enough to work with the pastor. We entrust several church tasks to leadership and perhaps with good intentions. However, these positions, as is all positions in the church, must be filled with anointed men and women of God, rather than men and women with just natural talents and abilities. The Nones and others who become discontented may feel the pressure of committing to a ministry when they don't understand the principles of God's Word concerning finances, and they suspect a mismanagement of funds.

It is vitally important that every member understands God's principles concerning their individual finances as well as the finances of the church. Many people have left the church because of a misunderstanding in this area. They may feel the church leadership has made decisions that cause them to feel pressured in this area. There must be teaching on the principles of giving, in faith, believing that God desires that His people walk in success in every area of life, particularly in their finances.

When the finances are not self-sustaining, the church resorts to other means of raising money. Many times, we develop excessive programming to raise needed finances. Are there too many programs? Is fellowship the motive or are we trying to raise the monies that should be given in tithes and offerings? What is the current financial state of affairs? The more important question is: What is the current state of affairs relative to the prosperity of our souls?

Beloved, I wish above all things, that thou mayest prosper and be in health, even as thy soul prospereth.
III John 2

The Bible addresses these issues by revealing to us the wisdom of obedience to God. God's intention is that the church be wealthy; a place where every need is met, both physically and supernaturally. Leaders must ensure that their members are equipped to handle the responsibilities of finances in their homes as well as the church. After all, the believers are on display, showing the benefits of becoming one of

God's own. We are a royal priesthood with an inheritance from Father God, who gives the best gifts to His children. The Word explains how to build and manage funds by understanding the tools used to obtain our needs and desires.

Money, Money, Money

Most of us have been taught to place our trust in money. We see it as though we will not be able to purchase or receive what we need or desire from it, so we hold on to it tighter than life itself. The wrong emphasis has been placed on its ability to do the things in the world we need it to do. It is baffling how the world acknowledges the money system, despite the fact that the words *In God We Trust* are so boldly written on each denomination of currency.

Money really has no power in the Kingdom of God, other than as a tool we use to meet financial responsibilities. Kingdom children attain their needs and desires from God; we are not dependent on the world because God is our provider. That is where many individuals may have misunderstood the Word of God when sermons were preached concerning believers' needs. We must understand that God is our sufficiency and in Him do we place our trust.

The Church must assure new members receive the proper teaching relative to not only finances but the principles of giving, sowing, reaping, faithfulness to the local church, as well as to individuals. Principles of loving and sharing with others, the Word of God, and the love of God will cause us to handle our finances and our time properly, and increase our faith in Jehovah Jireh.

Money, spiritually speaking, is such a small thing; it is a tool used in the world. Money is described in the Bible as a means of defense and is used as such. Money comes, money goes, it purchases temporal things. The Church uses it as a means to an expected end; not a supernatural end. Many congregations will need to change their way of thinking about money and realize that the church needs to be taught in this area of handling money as a means to reach an expected end.

Money gives us a false sense of security. We have all heard how God can blow on money and it's gone. Money is simply a means of exchange for worldly goods. My father once said, "The attainment of money was easy. Getting money easy? Yes, because it all depended upon what you were willing to do to get it." He meant that if you had some boundaries, whether moral or ethical, it would stop you from attaining it. But if your focus was on just getting money, no matter what, then you could do whatever was necessary to get it. Subsequently, it was just a means of exchange. It was a tainted and harsh perspective, but it was true.

Our pastor told us a story he had heard one Sunday about another pastor giving his congregation good and bad news: The bad news? The church was broke. The good news? The money was in the pockets of the congregation. Where is the church's money? In our pockets, we are just not willing to give it.

The local body has been operating in this area of finance with erroneous information. Members of congregations are attempting to reach success in their finances with (1) an expectation without the proper foundation or (2) expecting output without the proper input of data. Many members do not realize that money, in and of itself, has little to do with the success and prosperity of the church. Believers of the local body operate in faith. We receive from God because we practice the Word of God based on godly knowledge, godly principles, and the application of godly Wisdom. The attainment of money is just the first step. You can have money and be treated unfavorably as if you did not have it. You can have money but cannot exchange it for intangible things, such as not having a mind to give of your finances, not sharing time, and definitely not sharing the Word of God. Therefore, you may not understand the wisdom of the concept of giving.

Giving

No other area are we more challenged in than in the area of finances. The local body and its members, operating as an "organism," should make every attempt to operate in transparency and faith. A local body usually will not have difficulty with its members giving when the operations are transparent. However, a local assembly where its members are unaware, where leadership misuses the funds for personal agendas, will soon find themselves in conflict with the body of committed believers. Some believe that the pastor of a local assembly should have the flexibility to carry out his visions and agendas without a lot of explanation. However, there are many incidents of church disorder and chaos which cause individuals not to believe in giving. Leaders need to understand that there must be a balance in the decision-making process of handling finances. The congregation understands this to be oversight by a finance committee, whether it be the trustees, deacons, or an executive board consisting of impartial congregation members.

The handling of finances requires great faith and spiritual discernment. Governing bodies assisting the pastor must have good decision-making skills relative to expenditures within the body. The body, the sheepfold, entrust these leaders to keep the enemy at bay, as well as build the local assembly upwards spiritually, meet the needs of the community, and carry out the Great Commission God has given them. Wow, it is a huge responsibility! The Apostle Paul expressed to Gaius the extension of love and kindness toward other churches in Macedonia. Paul spoke of the liberality of giving and sharing the Gospel and operating in an honorable manner. Does this Scripture come to mind?

For if there be first a willing mind, it is accepted according to that a man hath, and not according to that he hath not.
II Corinthians 8:12

The basis of gaining favor is interdependent with our giving. John 3:16 explains the importance of giving. If God gave His most precious gift, how about us? Upon joining the local body, this area should be discussed to give new members foundation concerning finances. A lack of knowledge and strong faith will lead to a mentality of mistrust. Lack of trust in leadership (in the natural) will lead to a lack of trust (spiritually) in God and therefore, lack of faith. Without faith, it is impossible to please God. This is how the cankerworm enters the minds and hearts of people. Without giving, you will never understand a concept of favor.

Favor

We then move to the third step of favor. We receive favor as believers because of our daily walk with God. Favor is brought about by giving and by practicing His Word. As we exhibit His Holy Spirit, others see the goodness of Jesus as a sparkling jewel. We are kind, longsuffering, patient, forgiving, loving, compassionate; our attitudes are of gratitude. We are thankful and faithful to God. We have learned how to walk in favor to receive favor. Therefore, we obtain our needs and desires from God.

A Wealthy Place

It is a wealthy place where success and prosperity meet. Wealth requires a supernatural climb because you must be settled in your faith. When we increase our faith using the Word of God, we arrive at a place of wealth. When you are wealthy, you are healthy, because you understand the supernatural means of exchange. Every need and desire is met without the sweat of your brow. You have been so saturated in faith in God that you now have the abundance, the exceedingly more, and you did not have to work hard, steal, or kill to get it. It is your inheritance from a loving and giving Father, just because He loves you. So, when miracles happen, we can say, "God Did It."

Therefore, we obtain our needs and desires from God. We are wealthy because we receive what we needed when it was not within our means to attain. We arrive at a wealthy place when somehow our problems are unexplainably resolved. You know you are in a wealthy place when you receive something or everything that according to the worldly standard, you were not supposed to attain! When miracles concerning areas in our lives occur, we then walk in a place where we believe everything is possible, and we have no limitations because God Did It!

Thank God, the Church of our Lord and Savior will never be dependent on the operations of man nor man's finances! The Word of God tells us that the Church of our Lord and Savior will always remain and the gates of hell will not prevail against it. We need to understand that God is watching our obedience to His will; our increase and prosperity depend on it. The power that God has entrusted to us, to heal and deliver, the school of teaching us to love, should never be in a state of illness. Generally, challenges for individuals in the area of giving are due to a lack of trust in the handling of finances.

CHAPTER 7

THE CANKERWORM

Finances in the church must be responsibly handled. Otherwise, the financial standing of the local body will be challenged. The leadership responsible for handling the business matters of the local assembly must be equipped with basic foundational education and biblical principles. The Cankerworm has no backbone and does not like light. If we look at this animal figuratively, we can apply it to what happens in the local assembly. Leaders without foundational principles in handling finances will not have any enlightenment and may cause blunders in the area of finances. Whether mishandling budgets, overextension of responsibilities, or a lack of congregational giving, the finances of the church can prevent the local body from being financially sound. When this occurs, it may cause them to resort to alternative ways of obtaining money.

Church and State Separation

Many pastoral leaders resort to applying for government grants and programming to facilitate the lack of tithers. Leadership often lacks the understanding of grant accountability; they think they have the power over how the money will be spent, changing budgetary line items to allow the flexibility and handling of church funds. Most do not understand the manageability, accountable reporting, and consistent search for sustainability. Most just want someone to write the grant, with little or no understanding of the federal regulations the church must abide by. Then the church, however, will no longer enjoy the separation of the church and state relationship.

Financial Improprieties

There are other financial improprieties which have caused individuals to question the activities of the local body. Some churches have even been found "cooking the books," and some have been found not keeping records at all. It stands to reason that when the public hears of such affairs, it causes people to shake their heads and a "seed" to not trust the church is born. Understanding the perception of a church's lack of integrity and improprieties should cause those in charge of financial matters to be very careful how they handle funds. Years ago, we would shun the very appearance of evil and not bring a reproach on the church.

Some activities have drawn the enemy to attack the pastor and members of the local body. Predators watch as pastors hand over briefcases to "armor bearers" to carry when his arms are perfectly strong enough to carry. Ironically, when this occurs on the outside of churches, and the Armed Robber is watching, it causes him to reason that there must be a lot of money inside; it would be tragic when they grab it, or someone gets hurt, and there is no discovery of a briefcase full of money. They watch many habits of today's church leaders and marvel at the resemblance of their activity to that of con artists or common criminals with no integrity, and the propensity for deceitful pastors is seen as fair game. Some pastors watch for individuals who have given to many churches and those who have the ability to financially support the visions and programs of leadership. In some cases, a courtship begins. If you are a large contributor, you may become a victim of predators right in the church. There are many activities that can cause a breach in God's protection because we step outside of the realm of God's Word.

> *But ye are departed out of the way; ye have caused many to stumble at the law; ye have corrupted the covenant of Levi, saith the Lord of hosts.*
> Malachi 2:8

If we practice the law of love, the law of giving to others, and the law of faith, we will not stumble in our efforts to teach and reach others.

Building of the Expensive Temples

David desired to build the most extravagant temple for the Lord; he loved God so much, I believe David would have created the most beautiful edifice imaginable. However, God gave instructions to the contrary. Are we getting instructions from God when we determine to build temples today? We should compare the cost of the overhead to the number of people we could feed or house for the same amount of money. The homeless, orphans, healthcare facilities, soup kitchens, and the like may be more beneficial to the mission of the church. Are we really building in the hearts of men; or placing a yolk on our members' necks. The costs associated with extravagant buildings may cause the assembly to need members who have not yet joined or committed to financially support these endeavors and create the inability to really get to know the people and their needs. It may result in excessive programming, conferences, and other fundraising events to entertain the people and raise funds. In addition to the financial struggles are the salaries and contracts. Yes, these situations all have the possibility of causing people not to want to be a part of that particular project.

God adds to the Church based upon the spirituality of the local assembly and not according to the best choir, the most beautiful building, or the most popular pastor. Unfortunately, the church's report card is graded by people. Whether successful or unsuccessful, the community will base its opinion in accordance with whether the local body is "fishing for souls" and whether they are meeting the needs of the community.

Large buildings bring large mortgages, gas, light and energy bills, taxes, insurance, and maintenance; and these can strain our spiritual relationships just as they may in our individual lives. The church begins to feel the pull of Satanic attacks when we cause a breach by placing ourselves where God never intended. Why? We stray from His precepts, His principles, and mostly from the obedience of His Word. The Scriptures tell us to tithe (Malachi 3:10), give (Luke 6:38), and be a generous and cheerful giver (II Corinthians 9:7). Trustees often look for ways to stay within the budget by cutting costs such as limiting programs in the evening or looking at limiting the number of days the church is open on a weekly basis. Deacons and trustees look at business aspects of the organization, as opposed to remembering the local assembly being blessed by God and operating as an organism. Again, we should ask ourselves, "Does the success of the church lies in the hands of its congregation?"

What individuals need to know is that God loves His Church and where God blesses, He makes every provision for that local assembly and its members. He adds financially as well as spiritually, and He causes them to bless others. In other words, as the Shepherd is blessed, His sheep are also blessed.

Some ministries will proudly attest that the salary and benefits of the pastor must be paid, regardless of the bills being paid. However, we have heard of stories of those who are not concerned with the church assets nor its liabilities. Again, for those looking in from the outside, this scenario does not look good. We must remember that we are examples before others and they may see individuals of this type as stumbling blocks. Some spiritual leaders will disagree, but seemingly, since we know that a large group of people today do not want to be affiliated with the church, we should at least attempt to address these issues.

Church Payrolls

It has been traditional to have the pastor and musician on the payroll. Over the years things have changed. Now practically everyone who is instrumental in conducting the service wants to be paid! One of the traditions, many hope we will continue to adhere to, is to maintain a balance in the amount of the annual budget contributed to the payment of salaries in the church. Traditionally, the pastors had full-time jobs and supported their own families. Later, some organizations felt a responsibility for providing for the living expenses, care for the pastorate house, and transportation. Just how much should the church be responsible for? In our zeal to show our affection towards the pastor and others, we must maintain balance in these areas of expense. Does the local body have the ability to pay for expensive cars and homes?

Leadership should assure a level of reasonability, especially when comparing the church expenses in salaries to the amount of benevolence paid to those in need. Should we pay the camera man, media workers, guitar player, drummer, organist, and pianist, pastor's secretary, church secretary, maintenance workers, and others until we pay out more that we take in? Are the wages out of balance? Ministry leaders, what happened to the calling on our lives and our willingness to do what God asked us to do (unpaid)? Many of us know that love offerings and perhaps other offerings are acceptable and biblically based. How far should this go in modern times? Again, the idea causes us to operate as an organization and in some areas corporations, like a business rather than an organism. No one commits to these tasks as a part of their ministry to help others, although it is God who gave the gifts and talents. God blesses those of us who exercise our gifts to others in many ways: He blesses our finances, our health, and our wealth based upon what we freely do for His Kingdom. Our reward should not always be from the church's payroll, but from heaven. We cannot purchase our way in or work our way in, but only through love, the blessing of God's people and the Kingdom work.

We often forget that God Himself commands that we go out into the world to make disciples, using our gifts and talents. As a part of our joy in the Lord, we labor and rejoice in the building of the Kingdom of God. It is our priority to use our gifts, talents, and abilities for the furtherance of the Gospel, not to make money as a part of our endeavors to be comfortable. We forget the suffering cost of living this Christian life while working for God.

> *Brethren, present our bodies as living sacrifices;*
> *holy and acceptable unto God which is our reasonable service.*
> Roman 12:1

God returns everything the cankerworm caused to be lost, **Lest We Stumble.**

CHAPTER 8

THE IMPORTANCE
OF THE HOLY SPIRIT

**The Holy Ghost keeps you from doing everything wrong and
teaches you how to do everything right.**
Kim Austin

Most of us reach a definitive moment when we realize that we need God. It is then that we must submit to the Holy Spirit, the Comforter whom Jesus Christ left for us to be empowered to do the will of the Father. At the moment that you really begin to seek God and His will for your life, you will seek His face as you have never sought Him before. You will develop a hunger and thirst to be close to Him and to commune with Him in the early morning hours.

I love them that love me,
and those who seek me early shall find me.
Proverbs 8:17

When your spirit intensifies, your focus will totally turn to Him; then you will know that you have reached the moment when your innermost desire is to please Him in the beauty of Holiness. When this happens, your response to His voice will be "Yes, My Lord." His call, His work, and His perfect will becomes a priority in your life. You begin to think of others more than yourself; you esteem others higher that yourself.

The Lord hath appeared of old unto me, saying,
Yea, I have loved thee with an everlasting love: therefore with
lovingkindness have I drawn thee.
Jeremiah 31:3

New Believers in Christ

Another fragile relationship in the local assembly is the new person to the church or "the babe in Christ," who comes to the church for a different life, but has not learned how to live the converted lifestyle. These persons have already been subjected to hurt and disappointment, and do not need someone mishandling them. They have already been exposed to every trick and every con. They have stolen, lied, cheated, been truly bruised and beaten, and their way of escape may have been through drugs and alcohol or other addictions and negative behaviors. Many have committed all manner of sexual immoralities, perhaps to survive and care for their children. They may have been kicked out of their families and lost all friendships. Quite frankly, when they come to church, they come for a difference. They want positive change, not more of the same.

These souls are looking for another chance. They are looking to be loved. They want to be reunited with their estranged family. They are looking for Jesus because it is Jesus who has drawn them with lovingkindness. They are looking for unconditional love that understands and accepts their flaws and faults. They must be gently taught and gently handled. As leaders, we would do well to realize that God Himself has drawn them to our surroundings and placed them in our care.

Receiving the Holy Spirit

Dictionary.com defines *mourning bench* as a bench or seat at the front of the church or room, set apart for mourners or penitent sinners seeking salvation. The mourning bench is indicative of private confession and

repentance. When we accept the blood of Jesus Christ, our past and our sins become dead. Our former lives are replaced with the joy of the Lord through the indwelling of the Holy Ghost. These days it is not required that an individual physically be seated up front; no need to embarrass them. However, the mourning bench symbolizes the newcomer being focused on the Word, removing distractions from the message, and observing every move of God. Members of the church can pray for newcomers, take them under their wings, and keep watchful eyes on the newcomers' spiritual needs and growth.

Sitting up front on the mourning bench is symbolic of being up close and personal with God through prayer, supplication, confession, and repentance; which is necessary for the conversion and regeneration process. When a babe in Christ is in this situation, that is a fine time for one of the mothers of the church to intervene, assist with spiritual growth, and help birth out that soul. Instruction must be given with kindness and patience until the person is strong enough in the Lord to eat the strong meat of instruction, reproof, and rebuke. Most reproofs and rebukes will come through learning the Scriptures. Others come from mature Christians and church leaders to teach instructions unto righteousness. Remember, the newcomer has been immersed in the ways of the world, and those worldly ways must be destroyed, especially those that have become strongholds. Spiritually speaking, "Flesh must die!"

So then they that are in the flesh cannot please God.
Romans 8:8

The pastor and the leadership inherit the responsibility to train in the image of God and protect the spiritual growth of new Christians until they have heard enough of the Word to be rooted and grounded in strong faith. When newcomers share the pews with us, they bring their weaknesses and may need church leaders to discern that the Holy Spirit has drawn them and that they need to come to an altar of prayer and confess that something has touched their hearts. We need to welcome and encourage them with outstretched arms.

New babes are on pablum (soft baby cereal with little taste), and it may be a while before they can drink the sincere milk of the Word. They have to be nourished with the cleaning springs of living water, the Holy Spirit. Some churches have a tradition of assigning either church mothers or elder brothers (along with the pastor) to nurture new babes in Christ.

People develop over time, and they become what they are fed. The delicate process of "loving in" a person into the Kingdom should be the top priority of leaders. Even when they join an auxiliary ministry of the church, God is not through with them yet just as He is not through with us. We are all being molded by God into the image of Christ. Young Christians may not be able to carry out a task in the church as well as someone else who has years of experience and reliance on the Father, but if they have a love and zeal to try and work out their soul salvation through sanctification, let them serve in some capacity within the church.

Working It Out

Whether a new member, returning member, or a repentant backslider, God and the angels in Heaven rejoice when you come (back) into the fold and show maturity as a believer. Many mature believers can remember the lessons, tests, trials, and tribulations of working in the kitchen and the choir. God can use these ministries as testing and training grounds to prepare people for future ministries and missions. As mature and strong believers, we must realize that we are the pillars of the local assembly and must be able to help these soldiers along. We should treat them as sisters and brothers who are part of God's family. Our local assembly will have matriarchs and patriarchs leading the family in holiness and love. The leadership team would carry this soul until the conversion and regeneration process is completed, so he will not be swayed by the storms of life nor the blowing of the wind and every doctrine. Give him time and opportunity to learn to be sober-minded until he learns how to keep the Word in his heart while his mind is renewed in Christ Jesus.

> *That we henceforth be no more children,*
> *tossed to and fro, and carried about with every wind of*
> *doctrine, by the sleight of men, and cunning craftiness,*
> *whereby they lie in wait to deceive;*
> Ephesians 4:14

Jesus' love has set the example and given mature believers an understanding of how to treat other and how to handle newcomers to the faith. We should remember the mindset of Christ when He said,

> *But Jesus said, Suffer little children, and forbid them not,*
> *to come unto me: for of such is the kingdom of heaven.*
> Matthew 19:14

Newcomers to the faith are similar to babes or children because they have just been born again, and our perception of them is as newborn babes. You would not give strong meat to a newborn babe; you first establish a bond of love. Then nurture the babe, just as a baby, gradually feeding them in love. Discipline does not come until they have been taught, tested, and tried by situations in life. They receive the gift of baptism with water and fire with the Holy Spirit being the comforter, keeper, and teacher.

Once established, rooted, and grounded, newcomers may be able to stand the wind blowing, the rain, and the storms of life. They have learned that if and when they transgress, the repentance prayer is there for them. God will forgive them and cleanse them from all unrighteousness (I John 1:9).

"Ouch, it hurts!" - Lifting a Godly Standard

Another growth spurt of maturity occurs when believers understand that God chastens those whom He loves, so chastisement will come during times of spiritual development. Mothers of the church who are mature in the faith and have established a loving relationship with the "babe in

Christ," who has carried that soul in supplication and prayer, is now also able to rebuke and reprove when they know the babe, now a child, has been taught and understands, bur are not acting in accordance with the Word of God.

> *All scripture is given by inspiration of God,*
> *and is profitable for doctrine, for reproof, for correction,*
> *for instruction in righteousness:*
> II Timothy 3:16

When a fleshly mindset causes a person to get upset by instruction or rebuke, the enemy will attempt to make them angry enough to leave the Church, which is the very place where God has given them safety. If you have not invested in a person, developed a relationship, and helped a person along their spiritual journey, then your instruction, rebuke, or reproof will more than likely be offensive to them. Babes in Christ are already being drawn and sent to an assembly where their spiritual growth can increase in knowledge, truth, faith, and love. If they are not yet ready to receive information from you, then you may do more harm than good and cause the person to stumble which can also cause you to stumble.

John 15 delineates the requirement for success in living the Word of God.

> *Now ye are clean through the word which I have spoken unto*
> *you. Abide in me, and I in you. As the branch cannot bear*
> *fruit of itself, except it abide in the vine; no more can ye,*
> *except ye abide in me. I am the vine, ye are the branches:*
> *He that abideth in me, and I in him, the same bringeth forth*
> *much fruit: for without me ye can do nothing.*
> John 15:3-5

If you have abided in Christ and Christ in you, you will bear fruit. Without Him, you can do nothing! If there is no rescue team, the pastor becomes too busy; and the church mother does not know how to travail for a soul. Without their wise counsel and mentorship, the babe will remain carnally minded and keep one or both feet in the world. This new baby will be aborted at the hands of the Church itself and the hungry baby who has professed Christ may not get another opportunity to possess Christ. These individuals will quickly identify the church as being in the same condition as the world, with the same type of spirits of the world. They will think that the church looks, acts, tastes, sounds like, and resembles the world.

The new convert's appetite for "something different," is not satisfied, until perhaps the next occasion that they decide to return. If they perceive that the church has nothing different to offer, they will be drawn back to their old ways, old friendships, and unfortunately, old lifestyle. Sometimes we, the church, will get another chance to minister to these babes but sometimes we won't. It is this pivotal place that we cause them *to stumble and in our error, Lest We Stumble as well.*

CHAPTER 9

TRADITIONS, RELIGIOUS PRACTICES, AND CHURCH ETHICS

Thus you nullify the words of God
for the sake of your tradition.
Mark 7:13 NIV

You hypocrites! Isaiah was right when he prophesied about you:
Matthew 15:7

Jesus made it clear that godly traditions have been misinterpreted and become the "traditions of men." No tradition or religious practice is above the authority of the Word of God. Teachings, church ethics, and even the soul-stirring music should be in alignment with the Scriptures.

The lyrics to a favorite song of mine, says:

I like the old way of preaching and pray'n, I like the old-time way,
I like the old way of singing and shoutin', I like the old-time way
(Author Unknown)

The song sung by the late Bishop G.E. Patterson reminded me of the old-time way; I call it tradition and yes, religious. When I hear this song, I remember the importance of the old-time way; it was sure and true. What I am saying is that the old-time way reached my heart, caused a desire to get to know God, created a hunger and thirst for God, and a conviction of the sin in my life. It taught me how to call on the Lord, to obey, and how to pray fervently. It made me want a change in my life; it just pierced my soul. Every now and then, a leader will break out with one of those 'ole time' songs. Why? It worked! We learned how to trust and believe the ways of God based upon the Holy Scriptures.

Today, we hear an echo that tradition and religious practices are outdated. When we separate ourselves from our godly traditions, religious practices, and customs, we may destroy the very teachings of family values and principles that brought unity in the family and the spirit of unity into the local Body of Christ (the church). Christian values were taught and yes, adhered to, by family members, church members, and the community. Perhaps we should examine the definition of these terms for a better understanding before we decide to throw these practices and traditions away like a pair of old shoes.

Webster defines the following:

1. *Tradition* – an inherited established or customary pattern of thought or action or choice; the handing down of beliefs and customs, by word of mouth, by example, without written instructions.
2. *Ritual* – the established form especially for a religious ceremony; a system of rites; a ceremonial act or action; a customary repeated act or action.
3. *Religion* – the service and worship of God or the supernatural, devotion to a religious faith. A personal set or institutionalized system of religious beliefs, attitudes, and practices. A cause, a principle, or belief held to with faith and order. Religious practices derived from the statutes, laws of nature.

Some practices can be contrary to God's expectations and usually, decisions made by man. These types of religious practices perhaps need to be changed. The Godly traditional religious practices understood in the proper context were developed so the local body would conduct themselves in the manner God expects; from the example of Jesus Christ, those things that resemble God. What became problematic was how Scriptures were interpreted and whether the revelation of God was sought by leaders and whether received through the inspiration of God.

> *For who hath known the mind of the Lord, that he may instruct him? but we have the mind of Christ.*
> I Corinthians 2:16

Perhaps through the decades, we have lost the original meaning of God's intentions, traditions, and practices, but there is a need for a standard when leading a group of people. If we closely study I Corinthians 2, we may gain insight into understanding the spiritual wisdom of guiding our traditions and values versus the traditions of men.

Traditional Services

The history of a church is very important. How we conduct weddings, homegoings, revivals, and various ceremonies has been taught generation to generation. Understanding the dynamics of that particular denomination and the rationale for changes is equally important for current leadership. Therefore, all documents relative to changes in the ministry, pastors, and financial documents should be kept in a safety deposit box. Documentation of policy implementations and the purpose for changes will impact a body of believers. Who and why changes were made, organizational changes and the rationale for changes should be reviewed with the assurance that it parallels the Holy Scriptures. Church splits and denominational changes will often occur because of the traditions of men. These events are important to the local assembly years or decades later. Have you ever wondered why certain policies or procedures are in place? Even in the Bible, we have to understand the inspiration of God through the Holy Spirit, proper historical context, and spiritual significance distinguish spiritual from natural thinking, then God's revelation is manifested in the local assembly.

God inspires a Holy Spirit-filled vessel in the church to carry out a particular mission so that His purpose is fulfilled; it begins with a "sent" pastor. This is the reason for the development of inspired programming and inspired individuals being placed into leadership positions. God, through His Holy Spirit-filled vessels, is manifested to teach and reach others. If a non-Holy Spirit-lead vessel leads in his own ability and talent through the use of his own capacity, intellect, or popularity, then the overall goal of reaching and teaching others for spiritual growth will be lost. The sole purpose of being a leader is not to impress anyone or build the leader up but is to encourage others through ministry and train others through the submission of the Holy Spirit.

The purpose of all opportunities and interactions in the local body is for spiritual growth that God may get the Glory! Events such as Youth Day, Women's and Men's Day, and Mother's Day should be designed for special recognition and for enhancing loving relationships among the body of believers. We know that revival services are designed to invite non-attenders to service in an effort to draw them into the Kingdom, and to refill and revive those in the local body. These special services must be carried out for these purposes and not become ritualistic or as fundraising events.

Policies and practices are activities carried out to ascertain the success or failure of a method, to perform or meet an expected goal. If the policy or practice is successful, then that practice or policy may be adopted as the practice or procedure. If the percentage of success is reached, then the practice is performed regularly; thus, it becomes the way of doing things; some may erroneously title that practice as "religion" when it is a practice or procedure. An example of this may be the church covenant or church creed developed to identify how the congregation should behave.

Traditions are developed by the community to regulate behavior in that community. Written traditions become traditions because there is a need to regulate behavior to prevent crisis situations. Without inspired written procedures, practices, or statutes inspired by God, the crisis, which was the purpose of developing the practice, would be lost. Tradition has always been developed for the betterment of that particular community to prevent destructive types of behavior and more than anything, to honor God.

The world develops mores, folkways, and laws to govern immorality and for the protection of a group of people in a community. If these rules of conduct are not followed, chaos will result. Without the preservation and protection of godly traditions, these ideas, which are inspired, rooted, and grounded in agreement with the Word of God, confusion will arise in the local body. Rules, traditions, and religious practices are designed to divinely meet the needs of God's people in an ungodly world. Following a godly standard will keep us from being defiled from the world. James says:

> *Pure religion and undefiled before God and the Father is this, To visit the fatherless and widows in their affliction, and to keep himself unspotted from the world.*
> James 1:27

The teaching of godly values and principles is needed to support healthy godly character development. These values and principles were adhered to and formulated the traditional teachings of holiness. Some may call it the law or discipline, and some who were even offended by them call them offenses. Nonetheless, the intention was to develop godly character and to keep the local body from being defiled by the world.

Individuals are usually offended when you teach them to live a holy lifestyle. It is new, it is different, it causes them to be submissive to another in authority; they are after all "grown." Reasonable thinking may define an offense as an act by someone to intentionally do something to cause hurt or pain. When a person is told that they have done something wrong or offended you, you had the option to believe it was accidental and accept an apology or you could choose to be offended.

Learning how to treat each other in the church was instructional, you were being developed from a babe in Christianity so that your behavior could change and mature into godly behavior, comely to the Saints. Yes, behavior that resembles Jesus Christ, our Savior.

The most common battle between the old ways and the new is what the image of Christ should look like. When the world sees us, what do they see? What are the standards of the church and should they be followed?

Should they be taught? Some will agree that the rigidity of traditions and rules can cause a rebellious attitude. In order to prevent the people from leaving the local body or offending them, we sometimes compromise on many issues in the hope that the Holy Spirit will convert these souls. It is true that the conversion and regenerative processes are the work of the Holy Spirit, but are we still yet responsible for speaking truth, for teaching a standard to those who have never been taught the virtues of modesty, honesty, integrity, respect for authority, and other attributes of the Fruit of the Holy Spirit. So, who is responsible for teaching them and what is the best practice or method to teach in right way?

Traditionally, we did not have young pastors who had not been tried and tested leading congregations. We didn't have any who had not sat under leadership before they became leaders. Young pastors may have families who are not prepared to be seen as leaders. Wives may not be ready to allow the assistance of the church mother figures to assist them in their new calling. Today's pastors' wives do not want to hear from the mothers of the church and today's churches may no longer have dedicated committed mothers! Satan is able to move us off of prayer, and the power of the Church may be lost because we are now doing a "new thing."

Family traditions, values, and principles are taught through the institution of home. Modernists or Millennials want to get rid of what they call tradition. But what is it that they find wrong with traditional teaching and what has replaced it? Individualism? Perhaps they mean that we need to change some policies or practices which were developed by men. We are taught how to be good people and productive citizens by learning self-control or temperance, how to be respectful and considerate of others (especially those in authority), how to encourage and be motivated with initiative, and we learn how to be responsible for ourselves and others, and learn citizenship qualities.

Every need of the people was met. If you did not get breakfast at home, you could get it at church, and children attended Sunday School to learn about the Lord. Church ethics and etiquette were taught at the church; traditional values and principles of living a godly life, raising godly children, and making godly homes all came from the teaching of religious principles and traditions.

Blame for misgivings was not placed on others nor did individuals become dependent on others. Most individuals did not feel like someone owed them something, nor did individuals develop a sense of entitlement. Selfishness did not prevail. If something did not go right, the local body shared, cared, and helped many to persevere through difficult situations. Leaders of the church taught self-awareness, self-respect, and self-discipline. Character is developed through the traditions of home values and should be reinforced by the local church. If value for life or love for life is not taught at home, then where will they receive character development if not from the church?

Let's look at traditions we don't want to get rid of. We know of several. But if you are going to get rid of tradition, which ones are you going to get rid of and why? Are we to get rid of some or all? Which traditions and religious practices will cause us to stumble? Regardless of whether tradition, ritual, or religious practice, every action taken by leadership should be supported by the Word of God! Without the presence of the Holy Spirit (God), we can do nothing. Our manner and conduct should always reflect the Spirit of Christ Jesus.

Often changes need to be made; however, those changes must be Spirit led. When we look at the hurt and loss of power in the local church, we have to ask ourselves: Is it because the Holy Spirit's presence is no longer taking precedence in the local assembly but another spirit seems to be running things? The power in the Church traditionally was felt when you walked in the door. Those seeking forgiveness and deliverance ran into the arc of safety and the presence of God. There was a time that even the "traditional" wedding, baptism, home going, and christening services were desired by those in the community because they were sacred.

Practices

A practice is defined as an activity to do or perform, to carry out until proficient. I am reminded of an old adage, "Perfect practice makes perfect." If we can understand that we are practicing here on earth, striving for the *mark* ... the mark being the perfecting (the maturity) of the Word of God, perhaps we can have a better understanding of some of the religious practices which have been instrumental in forming church ethics. The inappropriate application by men and women on how to administer practices is what makes it impractical or ritualistic.

Many of the practices and religious customs or traditions are under attack by the younger generations. No longer is there a belief that one must be born again, or baptized with water and fire. The belief that the Holy Spirit is absolutely necessary in order to sustain the Christian walk in these perilous times has become a misnomer. Some may even ask, "Just how do you know I don't have the Holy Ghost?" Easy, we simply look at your lifestyle, and it becomes obvious.

We know that there is a need for order when maintaining an atmosphere conducive for God's presence. We must adhere to practices that keep the sanctuary holy. For instance, during prayer, it is distracting for members to hold conversations and be talking or laughing. It is not seen as a sacred time when this goes on. Worship and praise, choir rehearsals, and ministry meetings should always be regarded by the people of God as sacred times; even the things of God are not seen as sacred. When we consider every facet, every meeting is about a Holy God with holy assignments where souls are at stake. When we honor His presence in these scenarios, then we will restore the power and presence of the Holy Spirit dwelling within the walls of our church.

An example of the practice of selecting a pastor by a "Founding Family" has replaced the tradition of praying for God to send that local body a pastor. New trends have overridden tradition. Somewhere, someone decided to do it differently. Congregations felt a need for a young pastor to lead the youth; after all, they are the future (new thing). So, the traditional travailing and birthing out go out the window. We no longer believe in the power of the church (tradition). We even dare to pronounce and quote proudly, "The Holy Spirit is intelligent," as if the Holy Spirit is making these choices. Remember in the days of old when the power of God was prevalent, the members were not necessarily educated but had "mother wit." They exhibited common sense and spiritual discernment, but they prayed to God to be guided in their Christian walk and decision making.

We should understand that some practices are simply spiritual protection from viruses and infections to the Body of Christ. Think of the hospital Pre-Natal Unit. Much care is given, and protective clothing is worn for the sake of keeping a baby healthy. Thus, it is the same in the church. We strive to protect the babes in Christ by protective gear and protective practices to keep us from allowing worldly practices in church.

Procedures

Procedures are defined as methods to perform a task. Living for God and representing the Body of Christ is exhibited throughout an ethical system. God expects His organism to operate within guidelines known as church ethics and church etiquette. These guidelines are a fading mark in today's local assembly; a shadow. Some call it "a tradition." It is no wonder that many local assemblies have only taken a glimpse of these past traditions or rules, while some actively reject and remove them from their minds and no longer respect. Consider a moment and examine the value of church ethics and church etiquette: Were they developed from healthy, proven traditions and biblical standards?

Church Ethics

Church ethics may be defined as those behaviors which are in alignment with God's Word and God's standards, which are known biblically as statutes, ordinances, and commandments. Ethics are rooted in the ancient Greek idea of character. It involves doing what is right or correct and is generally used to refer to how people should behave professionally (and demonstrate individual ethics as well). Ask yourselves whose ethics are operating in your local assembly. Ethics tell us how to operate in our daily lives, and they are in agreement with God's Word and God's righteousness. Yes, times have changed, but we may not need all the tenets of tradition to change. We need men and women to change in accordance with God's ethical behavior. The behavior of the pastor and his leadership are seen as an example before his congregation. The home life, family finances, education, and concern for others are all in the spotlight. Whether leadership is seen as sharing information or caring for others, the congregation watches how these matters are handled. The pastor and his leadership's personalities must align with the Fruit of the Spirit, not look like or exemplify the world's standard. Are they arrogant, stubborn, and obstinate? Do they think of themselves more highly than others? All these issues may be alleviated by leadership following church ethics, Lest We Stumble.

CHAPTER 10

"MY WAY, YOUR WAY, GOD'S WAY"

*Jesus saith unto him, "I am the way, the truth and the life:
no man cometh unto the Father, but by me."*
John 14:6

**The Holy Spirit keeps you from doing anything wrong and it
teaches you how to do everything right!**
Kim Austin

If you have not embraced obedience, you will not like authority. You can see the manifestation of this in today's society. A lack of respect for authority has caused this country to exhibit a huge "behavioral problem child" for everyone. Individuals are so prideful that the requirement of humility that is so necessary for obedience is lacking in today's society.

Baby Boomers may remember Dr. Spock, a nationally acclaimed child psychologist who emphasized an attitude of thinking for oneself and self-expression. The 19th-century child psychologist advocated self-expression of children to their parents and believed that the children and teens were on equal levels as individuals who should be heard and that parents should compromise for the sake of peace. This idea may have been the beginning of disrespectful behavior which has greatly undermined authority in the home, school, and the church. Whenever there is no respect and honor in the home, certainly there may not be in school, in society, or in the church.

During corporate prayer, leaders must confess and repent of behaviors unbecoming of the image of Christ when dealing with others. Leaders must ask the Holy Spirit to search their hearts and reveal where they may have erred in their ministering; and ask God for forgiveness as well as forgiving others. We never know what a person has experienced in their hearts when interacting with the local church, the Body of Christ. There is so much turmoil in the world that we sometimes fail to see why a person has left us or why a person is not returning. Most of all, we fail to see the value of repenting to that person in a sincere manner. We fail to see the value of mending situations and are too quick just to say, "Let the Lord fix it," when we know we have not sincerely gone to the offending person and asked him or her if we can fix it. Our lips say, "Just pray for this or pray for them." Please don't misunderstand me; prayer is the best solution; however, sometimes our hearts are far from a heartfelt *I'm Sorry, Forgive Me Sister*, or *Forgive Me Brother*.

We don't even want to say, "God, you're right, and I'm wrong." Until we realize this process is a part of all of our regenerated processes, we will not be converted. Conversion means the new man is now in control and the old man is gone. Have you ever seen a person say, "I'm sorry," but continues to do that same thing again?

How does that "I'm sorry" make you feel? Eventually, you will not believe anything that person says.

The life of a leader is under a microscope by others and by God. Should we teach the principle that children should think for themselves and learn to make decisions? Yes. But with the understanding that their parents are the ultimate decision makers concerning the well-being of their children and children are to be obedient to authority. The premise is that they are right in their own eyes, rather than trusting that the authority figure is right and causing them to obey the authority. This is important in terms of getting the Word of God in you and being governed by the Word of God in your daily life.

> **Woe unto them that are wise in their own eyes,**
> **and prudent in their own sight.**
> Isaiah 5:21

Do you pray for your enemies with a prayer of reconciliation to mend relationships? Or do you use the world's philosophy of "feeding people with a long-handled spoon?" Do you lead the church in faith or do you just preach to the people to have faith? Do you tithe and give in the offerings? Or just ask the members to give more than you are willing in your finances? Do you govern yourself as an organization or an organism?

So many situations are overwhelming the minds of leaders. How much compromising must be done to maintain the role of our church membership? How much bending to programs and activities to draw our youth? Where is the Holy Spirit-led local body? What leaders should realize is that we draw those from out of the world with love and kindness, just like Jesus Christ. The task of drawing others will be hindered if they see the world and deceit in us. A con artist or gamer cannot be gamed; he sees deception because he is familiar with deception. In fact, he is presently acquainted with the master of deception. So, if a pastor or his leaders look worldly, as people initially are, they look at the motive in ministry. Even those who know your past will take a bit longer to truly believe the Word of God, particularly in the area of finances.

The Bible tells us to

> ***Abstain from all appearance of evil.***
> I Thessalonians 5:22

Appearances are important; how the world views members of the church is crucial to their understanding and submission to the Body of Christ. That's why we don't eat at the casino nor can we be seen at the liquor store or other places that will cause a reproach on the church.

> **Love is telling and teaching the truth;**
> **Deliverance is receiving it.**
> Kim Austin

CHAPTER 11

WALLS, WALLS, WALLS, AND DOORS!

What shall I render unto the Lord
for all his benefits toward me?
Psalm 116:12

Fulfil ye my joy, that ye be likeminded,
having the same love, being of one accord, of one mind.
Philippians 2:2

When the wrong leaders are placed in charge of a ministry, it may result in that ministry/auxiliary being closed to outsiders. The one door becomes a wall, and only those individuals behind the walls are qualified to carry out that particular task when there may be others equally gifted by God to help. We must always be open to our brothers and sisters in Christ, even if they are new in our midst. The leadership roles may need to be rotated and always open to spiritual discernment of what God is doing next. Mentoring a new member includes discovering their God-given talents and abilities. They should be able to work in that area while the leader and member pray to ascertain whether this is the ministry that God wants him to serve in.

In the meantime, they should be made to feel comfortable as the mentor leads and assists them in their development. Do not, however, treat them as children or as if they have no experience. Explore their gifts and talents, and teach them in a gentle manner. Many times, leaders in a particular group may isolate an individual, not realizing how territorial they have become by not making the new person feel included in the ministry.

As mentioned earlier, leaders must be prayerful and faithful to corporate prayer because they must constantly be guided by the Holy Spirit. We often forget about Satan and are not aware of spirits of jealousy, control, and competition that creep into our ministries of service. The leader of a ministry should be watchful and prayerful when others enter their ministry. They should find joy while they develop a person who is able to serve and grow in that ministry. God favors you; it is a "feather in your cap" when a new member makes a decision to join the ministry of serving. He is also solidifying his place in the Body of Christ, remaining in the body where he could have otherwise not returned or could have continued to sit dormant. You have been instrumental in their spiritual development if you have properly groomed them into discipleship. They are now ready to be an example to others, to love, to serve, and to encourage.

Conversely, if you have not gently taught with love and kindness, then you cannot take joy in being responsible for their growth. They could leave your ministry not wanting to serve anywhere else, not wanting to be a part of any other ministry, or feeling isolated.

As leaders, our focus should be on how we can serve the people of God. Pastors should pray about the instruction they are going to give to their leaders on serving with excellency. We pray that no division be found among us that will hinder the growth of the local body. In Philippians 4, there was a disagreement between Euodias and Syntyche. Their effectiveness was being hindered because of division, contention, and strife. The impact caused the powerful work they were engaged in to be hindered. The Apostle Paul quickly sent Epaphroditus to destroy the spirit of discord. Therefore, we must constantly pray together to guard our relationships with each other.

We don't want a relationship boxed in like four walls where no one else can get in. Our ministries should have an open door with three walls where the ministry of serving is a joy and not confinement. The door is not for members to come and go, or for a group that does not allow others in or out. The door is to show a willingness to invite all and be inclusive, allowing you to help out other service ministries, not be trapped by only those you like.

God is working on babes in Christ and trusts you to help in their development. Even if that particular ministry may not be their calling, the relationship should be one of love built upon them discovering their place in the church body. If they would like to try something else, we should assist them in transferring over into the ministry they may desire. Too often a person leaves a ministry with a bitter taste in their mouth. Regardless of faults or flaws, as leaders, we want to facilitate their growth and encourage them to stay in the overall Body of Christ. Your failure as a leader to identify satanic forces could cause you to cause them to stumble.

They come in with an expectation that healing and deliverance will take place in their lives, that they will recover, and that they can be helped. They do not expect to be mishandled, ignored, or unable to even trust the "hospital personnel." As leaders of God's Church, issues of trust, honesty, and integrity must be handled with Christ's love and honor. People should not go around or be subjected to being fed with a long-handled spoon, or afraid to speak their opinion, ask questions, and yes, even make mistakes. It is leadership that should understand that these are the steps of babies, children on milk being raised, taught and developed by God's shepherds and the leaders.

It is here, where some local churches filled with family and close friends in leadership, may hinder the growth. Bad relationship with one of "the family" may mean bad relations with all of the family and a person may become isolated, distrustful and eventually leave that place of fellowship. We must remember that Satan hates cooperation, and wants to destroy the Spirit of Unity within the body, no matter how small; it can cause a breach in the Spirit. When we are in leadership, it is an opportunity to mentor others and strengthen them to be soldiers in the Kingdom of God. One misnomer in the Church is that the elderly and the youth cannot work together, that they just can't seem to see eye to eye. That is nothing but a trick of the enemy. How can they be taught without a mature mentor in their area of ministry? Often you will see the blind leading the blind, therefore stumbling through their faith and love walks because they do not see the value of unity in the body.

> *Now I beseech you, brethren, by the name of our Lord Jesus Christ, that ye all speak the same thing, and that there be no divisions among you; but that ye be perfectly joined together in the same mind and in the same judgment.*
> I Corinthians 1:10

CHAPTER 12

PERILOUS TIMES

This know also, that in the last days perilous times shall come.
II Timothy 3:1

Where do we go from here? Realizing the needs of people and realizing the trouble we are facing in the church, I want to resolve that we must solve issues with the people. Spiritually, we traditionally subject ourselves to the workings of the Holy Spirit. The wickedness of the world requires the defense. The only spiritual weaponry effective towards the wickedness of the world is the precious gift God has left us for protection which is the Holy Spirit. We must clothe ourselves with the spiritual armor as depicted in Ephesians 6.

Finally, my brethren, be strong in the Lord, and in the power of his might. Put on the whole armour of God, that ye may be able to stand against the wiles of the devil.
Ephesians 6:10-11

Lifting Up a Standard

In looking at the purpose and the mission of the Church, we must review some of the biblical guiding principles and values. The Law of Moses, as outlined in Deuteronomy, is there to teach us strategies for living in this world, to keep us from the defilement of the world, and to keep us from adapting to the ways of the world. While it is literal in meaning, it is also a practical way of living. The practice of animal sacrifices for sin is no longer literal because we know that the blood of Jesus Christ delivered us from that requirement. But it does teach us that there are sacrifices that have to be made in this life in order to reach or attain just standards of living. No, we do not kill (in Hebrew, the Sixth Commandment means that you shall not murder when there is no legal justification for doing so), but it tells us that we should have a love for mankind, that we can sustain and open the door for forgiveness.

The Old Testament is truly for our learning and is valuable in the lessons of love for all men which is our Christian commandment. This is the requirement to obtaining our reward in heaven. We must love God and the things of God, love Jesus Christ, understand the gift of eternal life that He has provided for us, and love the precious gift of the Holy Spirit who keeps us in this world until our departure.

Can we see the need to change our agendas so that we may be more apt to teach and carry out God's Commission by preparing ourselves through natural and spiritual development? We must ask ourselves whether God has ordained us in this area. Do we possess spiritual discernment? Are we filled with the Holy Spirit? We don't want to be like the Sons of Sceva noted in the Book of Acts who attempted to cast out demons without the anointing of the Holy Spirit. The demons said that they knew who Paul was, and who the Christ was, but didn't know who these men were. The demons attacked the sons, who ran out naked and wounded. No one can deal with evil and wickedness without the person of the Holy Spirit. We must ask ourselves if we possess the Fruit of the Spirit. Do we have the interpersonal gifts? These attributes teach us how to communicate. In the natural realm, we must ask ourselves if we are educated about the types of mental illnesses that are so prevalent today and how they are discerned in the spiritual realm. Do we have the educational background required to counsel or treat these illnesses, are we legally qualified to handle mental health issues? Do we have the time and fortitude to counsel people throughout the process of healing or will we end up dropping them during a crisis because they have infringed upon our personal time? The church is almost the last institution that truly cares about healing the community, which is plagued with many problems.

As ministers, we may need to assess our qualifications and include the spiritual and natural resources to assist us in our roles. As we hit the streets, are we prepared to handle the crisis situations that will surely face us? I just ask that we, the church leadership, contemplate these issues. They are the issues of the non-existing home and are causing people issues in every institution across America. Only the Church has been commissioned to make better people and has the power to change people through the Holy Spirit. We need to assess our time and resources in this direction. The people perish without vision, and we all will stumble.

> *Wisdom is the principal thing; therefore get wisdom:*
> *and with all thy getting get understanding.*
> Proverbs 4:7

In all our getting, get understanding. Love is the essential requirement of the church. Every program, event, and activity must have the basis of love as its foundation. How can we love outside these four walls? How can we love inside the four walls?

I don't want to seem critical of the church or its leaders, but we must admit that these are perilous times and we will find ourselves asking, "What are we doing?" What is the best method of attaining the goal of teaching people that God loves them, despite everything? Everything else is secondary, so why have we tied and shackled ourselves with the wrong programs, the wrong itinerary, and the wrong leadership? It has caused us to lose focus and yes, stumble.

> *For other foundation can no man lay than that is laid, which*
> *is Jesus Christ. Now if any man build upon this foundation*
> *gold, silver, precious stones, wood, hay, stubble; Every man's*
> *work shall be made manifest: for the day shall declare it,*
> *because it shall be revealed by fire; and the fire shall try*
> *every man's work of what sort it is.*
> I Corinthians 3:11-13

We have various questions, so we must realize our purpose and determine what the church's priorities are. Can you really get people to desire the church family? Will new members come with a heartfelt willingness of mind to do the will of God and learn of Him? The Holy Spirit's presence is vital, and the presence of God must be felt through the workings of the Holy Spirit. It is Him who gives the desire to attend Bible study and prayer meetings and fast. Without a total commitment from leaders, we won't fast, and will not be able to really tap into the things of God and receive spiritual understanding. When we do not grow, the stagnation leaves an opening void of learning to end up depending on the secular things as opposed to learning about God. Yes, we will end up depending on our intellectual capacities and philosophers. We may become great orators with the ability to attract and make people feel good about themselves when we all may be missing the mark. The suffering way is to look at yourself daily. We like to feel good, we want to feel comfortable in our unrighteous ways, and rationalize our behavior. We must come to realize that God is right.

> *Examine yourselves, whether ye be in the faith; prove your*
> *own selves. Know ye not your own selves, how that Jesus*
> *Christ is in you, except ye be reprobates?*
> II Corinthians 13:5

Strategies

The church is or should be about developing people and the community. How do you win souls? Now that we have come to the conclusion that it is necessary and essential for the church to fulfill its mission, let's come up with some strategies. A very interesting book was introduced in marriage ministries a few years ago, known as *The Love Dare* (Kendrick and Kendrick, 2008). Later made into the movie *Fireproof* (Samuel Goldwyn Studios, 2008), the authors used biblical principles to restore a broken marriage doomed to divorce. The husband showed his wife unconditional love for 40 days, and it changed their lives and turned their marriage around to what God intended marriages to be.

Each of us should endeavor to engage one person in the community and show love no matter what. The bottom line is that the real draw for souls is accomplished when we meet people where they are, and give them the incentive to live a better lifestyle. In other words, our love testimony is a love dare because it will not be easy and requires us to give of ourselves more even if it is not reciprocated. It is time that we go back into the homes, help with children, and seek jobs for others. The challenge is whether we will be invited in. The question arises whether others will be willing to see life through the eyes of Jesus. We cannot force our way, but we can pray to be drawn to those in the community who need us most.

Money can help with Thanksgiving and Christmas baskets, soup kitchens, and second-hand stores where the homeless can get clothes. But these are temporary fixes, and after the eating is gone, people have no desire to be preached to, no need for Bible class, no want of fellowship. We must simply realize that our living testimony is the only true legitimate or effective draw. As the local assembly, we know the community (which is steeped in behaviors and philosophies of the world), has not been taught healthy, wholesome, or holy lifestyles. Inside the local assembly, the Word of God and the Holy Spirit in us may touch the hearts of our youth to understand that the church cannot compromise. The question becomes whether they will agree with the ways of the church. Unfortunately, it is only in crisis that we get the opportunity to minister to these individuals. However, new ideas such as dramas, interactive skits, and other programs will assist the church in these endeavors. In these areas, we can make an impact in the community. The church can request grant monies for intervention programs to teach faith-based principles while seeking sustainability and requiring mentorship programming. Just as we must work to stop fraud and violence in our communities, we must also educate our members and the community about the dangers of domestic and sexual abuses and call for an end to gang violence by retraining our young men.

The integrity and transparency of the Church must be realized. Church leaders need to take the lead in the development of rehabilitation clinics and programs. Drugs, alcoholism, and other substance abuses require intervention beginning in the home. Perhaps it is time to return to homes for prayer meetings. We realize that the drug problems in our communities exist because of the demand for drugs. Therefore, we may be able to lead youth to believe that they do not need to get high, and help them to no longer desire to escape reality, and give them alternatives to negative behaviors.

How can we convince young women that they don't have to settle for promiscuity, sexual immorality, and abuse? Will the younger women accept the teachings and listen to the older women? Can we teach younger women character and help them to develop godly values, morals, and principles? People are so oppressed that until we can meet them in their needs, they will not know that our God rewards those who diligently seek Him (Hebrews 11:6). This is our mission, *Lest We Stumble*.

CHAPTER 13

WHAT IS THE BIG ATTRACTION?

But whoever causes one of these little ones who
believe in me to sin, it would be better for him to have
a great millstone fastened around his neck and to be drowned
in the depth of the sea. "Woe to the world for temptations
to sin! For it is necessary that temptations come,
but woe to the one by whom the temptation comes!
Matthew 18:6-7 ESV

Why is there such a high rate of physical and spiritual abuse and violence in the world? We see signs everywhere that point to a lack of respect for life, lack of love, unkindness, and deceitfulness in the world. Christian values are not being taught in the world. One of my acquaintances inferred that ungodliness has come out of the closet and the church has gone in the closet.

So here is the playing field, and we must be readily trained with godly care which comes from godly knowledge and godly wisdom.

One of the most challenging assignments for the local church is keeping church members and ensure church retention. In our efforts to keep members, we find ourselves entertaining people instead of teaching them how to respond to the Word of God. This can be a major pitfall, leading to a slippery slope. Musical entertainment is usually the main drawing tool; that is why the music ministry is so important. People love to hear good singing; they love church for the wrong reasons. Music stirs their emotions, songs touch their hearts, they cry, but is that enough? Hopefully, the songs from the Music Ministry will keep them coming to church until they are rooted and grounded in faith. It is of the utmost importance of establishing a spiritual relationship with the Holy Spirit, your pastor, a mentor, and other mature Saints that they may grow into spiritual maturity.

The music ministry is vitally important, and part of the foundation of the local church. Souls are reached like electricity, and the power and presence of God are being transmitted and received from heart to heart. As God's music reaches the soul, it softens the "spiritual ground" to receive God's Word. If you have the strength to guard the Word in your heart, you will begin to mature and pass from the milk of the Word to solid food and spiritually "strong meat" (Hebrews 5:12).

The decision to change worship from devotional to praise can be beneficial to both the old and new members. Integration and balance in the worship service are important to the body and to the soul. Every person deserves the right to leave the Sabbath service feeling free, fresh, and fueled for the upcoming evening, week, or days ahead. Certainly, opening the Word (Scripture) and prayer have their places to lead us into praise.

What is absent is the embracing of each act; we find "the walls" spoken of in Chapter 6. Praise leaders should engage and support the deacons as the deacons embrace the praise service. Often these units pray alone, arrive only in time for their act and engage in their own agenda and forget to share with the others. Balance and support are of keen importance when young and old come together so that the perfect balance of God's presence is magnified.

The stirring of our emotions, the outpouring, displayed in many ways, builds an appetite for Word of God to become active in our daily lives which are submitted to the Holy Spirit. When we are saturated with the refreshing fire of the Word, it indicates growth and love of God, the things of God, as well as hunger and thirst for a relationship with God. The realization is that it is absolute essentiality is that we commune with God daily and receive His instruction on how to carry out the ministering needs to the world. This process makes us a ready vessel to labor for souls.

The Lost

A profound realization came to me when studying the Scriptures on the lost. It came to me that when something is really lost, we don't look for it. However, lost items in the Bible are portrayed as simply misplaced, and we should seek them out until we find them. It is valuable to us that we just don't accept that things (or people) are lost or gone. Instead, we should decide that they are simply hiding or is misplaced and waiting for us to find them. That revelation was awesome to me. So, we must seek the lost and aid Jesus in saving the lost. We have to attract people to God and the church with the same lovingkindness. Regardless of the attractions in the local body, we all agree that saving of souls must be the main attraction *Lest We Stumble*.

> *The Lord hath appeared of old unto me, saying,*
> *Yea, I have loved thee with an everlasting love: therefore*
> *with lovingkindness have I drawn thee.*
> Jeremiah 31:3

CHAPTER 14

A GODLY STANDARD

So shall they fear the name of the Lord from the west,
and his glory from the rising of the sun. When the enemy shall
come in like a flood, the Spirit of the Lord shall
lift up a standard against him.
Isaiah 59:19

Most people will agree that there must be a godly standard of conduct in the world. Failure to accept the standard in the local assembly causes leaders to compromise in many areas because they do not desire to follow tradition. The devaluation of traditional standards in the church takes us away from what God intended for His flock.

Do we really know who we are?

But ye are a chosen generation, a royal priesthood,
an holy nation, a peculiar people; that ye should shew forth
the praises of him who hath called you out of darkness into
his marvellous light;
I Peter 2:9

A light in the world, a city on top of a hill, Zion, a peculiar people, a royal priesthood, God's chosen people. That's who we are! We have been taught self-realization, self-preservation, and self-respect from the world perspective. However, we have not grasped the statutes, judgments, commandments, and decrees (the biblical principles) on how to operate in the world. We are led by the divine direction of the Holy Spirit. In interaction with others, some may exhibit Christ Jesus who is the way, the truth, and the life, while others are yet being developed to come to know and love our God.

While teaching five years of Criminology, one of the first lessons I taught was why people become criminals; then we looked at the characteristics of a criminal. We ended up discussing the many facets of character development. When we look at the institutions that have a hand in forming our character, we conclude that the foundation where values and principles are taught is in the home. When someone is raised in a home without love and nourishment, what development might we expect? It would be totally different than if they had been raised in a loving home where honor and respect were taught, and where these attributes were reinforced by the church.

Next, we go into the school system. The school system is an open population of young people, many underdeveloped. Now, the educational system has to teach not only academics but also social skills and acceptable behavior. Society unbelievably does not reward these for their worth! When an underdeveloped individual leaves an educational institution and goes right out into society, he or she may be highly intelligent but will be socially and spiritually depraved. Analyze the lives of some of our most notorious criminals, and you can see the vicious cycle. Biblically, we could say that these are the people filled with demonic spirits which can only be understood and dealt with by the church. But wait, there is no requirement to attend church like there is to attend school. So how does an individually come into the Good Shepherd's fold?

The Great Commission given to the church body is to go into all the world and make disciples. We should impact others with lovingkindness, and people should see Christ when they see us in our workplaces, schools, and communities. What they see in us impacts their decision to seek a relationship with God. Self-realization of who we are and what our basic needs are should be based upon who God says we are, rather than on thinking only of expressing an independence from standards and principles of godly living. Believing in Jesus Christ and His death, burial, and resurrection as the propitiation for our sins gives us salvation and assures our entrance into the Kingdom of Heaven. We must depend on God, and realize who He is and who He is to us.

Therefore I take pleasure in infirmities, in reproaches, in necessities, in persecutions, in distresses for Christ's sake: for when I am weak, then am I strong.
II Corinthians 12:10

Self-esteem is developed by clear, godly principles including those of responsibility, self-respect, and respect for authority. Our confidence, accomplishments, and creativity become successful when we depend on God.

I can do all things through Christ which strengtheneth me.
Philippians 4:13

As a part of the Body of Christ, developed through the love of Christ, we become companions with Christ; forgiving others, and showing the Fruit of the Spirit because we are the Body of Christ. Our safety in this world is based on our willingness to stand on the Word of God, which keeps us from snares, traps, risk, and harm. Pain and afflictions are light and short-term when we rely on and believe the Word of God. We don't become weary in well doing (Galatians 6:9).

For our light affliction, which is but for a moment, worketh for us a far more exceeding and eternal weight of glory;
II Corinthians 4:17

Many are the afflictions of the righteous: but the Lord delivereth him out of them all.
Psalm 34:19

Our physical needs are met by Jehovah Jireh, our provider (Genesis 22:14). The Scriptures tell us to be anxious for nothing (Philippians

4:6), to cast all our cares on the Lord (Psalm 55:22), and not to be concerned about what we will eat or wear (Matthew 6:31).

Wow, Wow, Wow! God has given us everything pertaining to life and godliness. We just have to listen, hear, and trust in the finality of His Word. If God says it, then it is so. Jehovah Shalom, the Lord is our peace (Judges 6:24). We are satisfied in life when we have the God's peace and when we know that we are abiding in the Holy Spirit to lead us in all things.

Our goal is to train the people of God until they resemble the image of Christ. We often hear the stories about "frying the fish before catching them." Well, in processing "fish," we also know there needs to be a proper cleaning utensil to clean the fish. Jesus said, "… with lovingkindness I have drawn thee…" (Jeremiah 31:3). The process of getting a babe from "the catching" to the "preserving," with salt and the cleaning with a knife prevents the fish from spoiling. Mature believers know that this process must take place; it is the process of sanctification and purification, with the fire of the Holy Spirit which removes all dross or impurities from our flesh and carnal minds; realizing that our bodies are the temples of the Holy Spirit, and our minds are transformed by the renewal principles of God's Word. We are being transformed and regenerated. Yes, the cutting hurts, just as when God chastises us and the Holy Spirit convicts us; it is very uncomfortable. However, it is necessary. But expect the enemy to bring condemnation, distrust, and contention to make you jump out of the process. You might feel offended; even though the intention is not there.

Offense is a term that many do not understand; it is used to cause contention and strife. When someone sets out to offend you, it is an intentional, not an unintentional act. When we don't like what we hear, or we hear something contrary to our own thought processes, we quickly allow the spirit of contention to convince us that we have been offended. We must be careful when receiving reproof and rebuke just as the person doing the reproofing and rebuking must understand how to reprove and rebuke in love. They can actually be transmitting loving instruction with the intention of helping us. We must be careful to receive the real transmission so that we do not erroneously perceive offense. Distorted messages have often caused many to leave the church or to be overwhelmed by a spirit of unforgiveness. People of God must strive to look for more positive perceptions and enhance communication with people. Sometimes they receive you, and sometimes they don't; thus, we can see the importance of the Holy Spirit being our guide in the handling of God's people and the things of God.

Training to the Image of Christ

There must be a godly standard. Do we have the world in the church because of compromising, or to keep our members, or to keep the tithes flowing? We intentionally try not to offend anyone, but we offend God when we compromise. Then what are you to say to these individuals who have heard the Word, seen the examples before their eyes, and still have not been converted? Some pastors prefer to teach on subject matters in the Bible, some preach the Word concerning sin, and some stick to topics of joy, love, and peace, but don't impart knowledge that the wages of sin is death. And heavens no! By all means, they won't preach about hell, talk about hell, or cover anything from the pulpit that does not appeal to or entertain the congregation. You may soon get a "We no longer need your service" letter.

Just how should we inform the unregenerated and unconverted that they must live the Word of God as well as hear the Word of God? They have heard the Scriptures, but not experienced change. After being around for a while, these members must gently be taught that it is time for a change. Of course, we are not speaking of newcomers to the church. Those individuals are drawn by our love and gently guided into the newness of Christ. But what do we do with those old babes that are still on milk instead of the strong meat of the Word? As leaders, we are responsible for informing them. Sometimes, we simply must tell them because we are not sure that they know. In that circumstance, personal counseling is called for. Ezekiel tells us we are responsible for telling them.

When I say unto the wicked, O wicked man, thou shalt surely die; if thou dost not speak to warn the wicked from his way, that wicked man shall die in his iniquity; but his blood will I require at thine hand. Nevertheless, if thou warn the wicked of his way to turn from it; if he do not turn from his way, he shall die in his iniquity; but thou hast delivered thy soul.

Ezekiel 33:8-9

CHAPTER 15

DON'T JUDGE ME! ... BUT I CAN SEE!

Examine yourselves, whether ye be in the faith;
prove your own selves. Know ye not your own selves,
how that Jesus Christ is in you, except ye be reprobates?
II Corinthians 13:5

Love is telling and teaching the truth;
Deliverance is receiving it.
Kim Austin

U sually, when rebuke, reproof, and instruction come to an individual, the normal comment is that "they are judging me." When a mentor in the church tries to impart a spiritual or natural discernment to someone, they are often accused of judging. It is true that the eternal judgment will come in times of the Great White Throne Judgment (Revelation 20:11-15), which will be the final judgment before the lost are cast into hell. The Gospel speaks that we should not judge each other. However, in this chapter, we are concerned with spiritual discernment and mentoring rather than judgment.

Once a *male* makes a decision to commit to the church, he or she is faithful and may only change this commitment when finances are involved. However, almost every *female* who leaves a church will make one of three complaints:

1. The congregation displayed "holier than thou" attitudes.
2. They wanted me to change my attire, but didn't God say to come as you are?
3. They treat some people differently, but God is no respecter of persons.

Women are concerned that other members are judging their behavior and appearance. Unfortunately, in some cases, it is true. However, the perspective that is missing is that leadership has not gently taught the person the process of change that will occur in the regenerated life. Baptism is symbolic of the newness of life in Christ Jesus, and old things are passed away; all things become new (II Corinthians 5:17). We are taught to examine ourselves before we participate in communion. We are also taught to examine ourselves when we see that our faith is not working for us. Often the discernment of the mature Saints can help these individuals, who simply, are sensitive and see the teaching of conversion and regeneration as judgment.

Seemingly based on Scripture, every person should look at their behavior and determine if they exemplify Holiness; "...Without such, no man can see God!" (Hebrews 12:14). Why do we get offended when others see our flaws and faults? When they bring them to our attention, why do we get mad? Perhaps we struggle with the old man and the ways of the flesh; perhaps the new man hasn't shown up in our behavior yet.

Therefore if any man be in Christ, he is a new creature:
old things are passed away; behold, all things are become new.
II Corinthians 5:17

Yes, we all will meet eternal judgment, but the use of spiritual discernment through the behavior we see now is a help to others in their spiritual growth. The Word of God tells us to teach others gently. Upon repentance and the receiving of the Holy Spirit, a change should have occurred. In the Book of Acts, Jesus spoke to Saul, and Saul was converted.

> *To open their eyes, and to turn them from darkness to light,*
> *and from the power of Satan unto God, that they may receive*
> *forgiveness of sins, and inheritance among them which are*
> *sanctified by faith that is in me.*
> Acts 26:18

Teach the acceptable ways of God in the spirit of love, and make a clear distinction of what behavior in the world looks like compared to what it looks like in the Kingdom of God. If you do not make this distinction, how will people know right from wrong?

Partial Scriptures are often quoted or taken out of context concerning judging others. The church must handle it gently and firmly when newcomers who are feeling judged inaccurately quote Scripture back to leaders. Here are some of the Scriptures that often confuse newcomers who do not know the whole Word of God and do not know how to rightly discern the Word of Truth (II Timothy 2:15):

> *Judge not, and ye shall not be judged: condemn not, and ye*
> *shall not be condemned: forgive, and ye shall be forgiven:*
> Luke 6:37

> *Judge not, that ye be not judged.*
> Matthew 7:1

We can discern without judging. We should respect the gift of spiritual discernment given to us by the operation of the Holy Spirit. God gave us the gift of being able to see with spiritual vision. We must respond or not respond to these visions as the Holy Spirit leads. Often people, especially young people, feel that they are being judged on their merits as individuals. In actuality, their mentors are not judging them in terms of heaven or hell, but are simply telling them what character they see, and basing their observations on what they would expect to see if looking at the image of Christ Jesus. We must look, see, think, and respond like Christ. The pastor, mentor, or leader is not judging you. He may simply be saying, "This is what I see through my spiritual eyes." He is exercising his gift of spiritual discernment. Remember, we often bring in the rudiments of the world and must fight to get the world out of the Church. In doing so, we must confess that we brought the world in.

> *And this is the condemnation, that light is come into the*
> *world, and men loved darkness rather than light,*
> *because their deeds were evil.*
> John 3:19

This, of course, does not apply to the initial encounters of new converts. After counseling, training, Bible class, and much prayer, newcomers to the faith must repent of sin and submit to the Holy Spirit, which will reveal who they are in Christ Jesus. What about those who are not new to the faith? There are members who have been in church for years, heard the Word preached and saw examples before them, but still have not been converted nor regenerated. We see tongue rings, new tattoos, improper revealing attire. The membership of the local assembly should ask questions to those who display these ungodly expressions of being in the world: What are you looking at? Who are you listening to? Young people are constantly on their cell phones and hesitate to obey instruction from the elders. Attitudes are not reflective of Christ, so someone must say something!

> *No discipline seems pleasant at the time, but painful.*
> *Later on, however, it produces a harvest of righteousness*
> *and peace for those who have been trained by it.*
> Hebrews 12:11 NIV

> **What you wear on the outside does not determine**
> **who you are on the inside; but what you are on the inside,**
> **will manifest itself on the outside."**
> Kim Austin

The World in the Church - Compromising to Keep

Decisions to accept imperfect behavior in the church have been made in an effort to appeal to the young people. We must also realize "tares" (Matthew 13:24-30) are being planted among the wheat of the church body and much of the world is coming into the church. However, we cannot compromise God's standards by making worldly provision for our youth, who are "fresh fish." Neither do we compromise our standards for the "stale and rotten" (those who have been in the church for years and still do not lead Godly lives). We must pray and demand in the spiritual realm that God bind the spirits of nonconformity and competition, and loose the spirits of cooperation and transformation so that we emulate the image of Christ Jesus. Our formula, spoken of by Paul in his letter to the Corinthian Church said:

Casting down imaginations, and every high thing that exalteth itself against the knowledge of God, and bringing into captivity every thought to the obedience of Christ;
II Corinthians 10:5

Verse 6 tells us what to do and how to handle attacks to our minds:

And having in a readiness to revenge all disobedience, when your obedience is fulfilled.
II Corinthians 10:6

Spiritual leadership requires us to pray and receive instruction so that we may choose the right people to work with our youth and our new babes in Christ. We want spiritually grounded mentors in leadership who have professed Christ and will lead our young people in pursuit of salvation. We must pray and commune with God every day and before every assignment. Putting the wrong people in the wrong leadership role may cause us to stumble.

Most young people in leadership have not experienced the Holy Spirit and are no match for the strongholds of the enemy. That is why the older Saints must teach the young. Even those who have attended church all their lives may not be mature in spiritual things, and thus, can be easily drawn by the pride of life to worldly things.

Do we really believe in life after death? Heaven or Hell? Do we speak of Heaven but not of Hell? Of blessings but not of judgment? What about the miracles we should be performing? Are we preaching and teaching to itching ears? (II Timothy 4:3).

The tool of music seems to be the first draw, followed by other activities that are attractive to the flesh. While it is useful to attract and minister in these areas, the church must exercise caution and care. The new language expressed in music and dance, as well as technology, is replacing pure and wholesome conversation. The strength of pure, honest, eye-to-eye verbal communication is essential. If you can't communicate with a person, how do you know how to commune with God? How can you focus on God with your cell phone in bed with you? How can you develop a relationship without displaying sincerity? How can you learn to desire love and develop trust?

Fellowship Leads to Relationships

The Word of God tells us that we are our brother's keeper and that we must love our brethren, be concerned, and help those who are poor in spirit, brokenhearted, and those captive to the darkness of sin. We can be part of many activities and ministries in the church. We can join the usher board, sing in the choir, sing like angels, pay our tithes and offerings, but have no charity in our hearts. If that describes us, we will miss the mark and not make it to heaven. What a catastrophic eternal judgment when God pronounces that we were playing church instead of believing in the Word.

The Scriptures tell us that relationships with others (those in the sheepfold) are vitally important if we want to please God. We can lose God's favor by the way we treat others. One of my friends made a very impacting statement to me once. He said: "Rules without relationship leads to rebellion." Many people simply are rebelling against the church, religious activity, and even God, because they have not developed a loving relationship with others and with God.

How can you develop relationship without assembling yourselves? I thought about this, and it is this reason I developed the survey and sought out responses from respondents of many demographics who did not regularly attend church. In a lot of cases, these were the people who were sick, bound, and lost.

Life is busy, and we have little time for ourselves, much less for other people. The art of relationship building is becoming a lost art. Many lifestyles are tormented by the pressures of life. Individuals are succumbing to depression, suppression, and other oppressions of the world, which is why they are in the condition they are in. Most have never been introduced to liberty in Christ Jesus or to the love of Christ, let alone being familiar with the mind of Christ and the Word of God. They may have never experienced the mind of Christ.

Those who attend our churches should be showing agape (unconditional) love. When you have the spirit of love in you and the indwelling of the Holy Spirit, people know it, feel it, desire it, and they want to commune with it! But how do you get to know the people you attend church with without having fellowship and getting to know them?

Through the process of praise and prayer, I learned how to commune with God. I began to understand His love for me. I became hungry for His Word. Whether it pertained to law or spirit, and even when it came through reproof, rebuke, and instruction, I just wanted to do whatever would please God. It was the love I felt that brought me to a state of humility and obedience. I wanted to hear from God, so I began listening to God through His ministering angels and the Holy Spirit. I obeyed those who God chose to help me in this Christian walk.

When people with their differences come to church, their experience must be one of love. In all our works, leaders must be mindful of this. We can work, serve, sing, have heart-to-heart communications, preach, teach, and use all the gifts God has put at our disposal. However, they must be carried out in love for the brethren, for strangers, and in our personal lives, personified especially with our enemies and those we don't like very much. When we don't show agape love, our leadership behaviors should be questioned. We must examine ourselves.

People come to the church expecting to be safe from the world and the issues that hurt them, bind them, or cause them to be lost. In many cases, they know their own condition, but they are not mature enough to know the condition of the spiritual hospital yet. They don't know that in the hospital, there are many patients with various diseases who are from various walks of life, are of different nationalities and that they all need a blood transfusion of the same type of blood:

J Positive.

CHAPTER 16

NOW, LET'S GO GET SOULS

Wherefore seeing we also are compassed about with so great a cloud of witnesses, let us lay aside every weight, and the sin which doth so easily beset us, and let us run with patience the race that is set before us, Looking unto Jesus the author and finisher of our faith; who for the joy that was set before him endured the cross, despising the shame, and is set down at the right hand of the throne of God.
Hebrews 12:1-2

I press toward the mark for the prize of the high calling of God in Christ Jesus.
Philippians 3:14

Outreach is no longer a secondary goal for the local church. It has become a primary goal for the Body of Christ. Let us be about our Father's business and go beyond the four walls. Carrying out the Great Commission to go into all the world and preach the Gospel to every creature (Mark 16:15) impacts our heavenly rewards. We have to deliver the mail, so to speak, that God has given us to deliver. Each of us must now show full proof of our calling, walking worthy of that calling. Let us first examine ourselves to see if we be in the faith. If so, it is time for intensive intercessory prayer. It is time to prepare the battle plan. It is time to pray and fast! So many of the enemy's strongholds have become prevalent because we have not fasted. The Scripture indicates that some spirits ONLY come out through prayer and fasting. So let's discuss some possible strategies.

Witnessing Teams

It is true that the best testimony is your own! Share how God brought you through tests and trials; you wouldn't have made it through without an active prayer life and prayer warriors actively travailing with the Holy Spirit on your behalf. Teams should have consistent, committed servant leaders and active prayer warriors, especially the church mothers who travail for the children and youth ministries as well as younger women and men. The local body may want to exchange event programming with true evangelistic settings that minister to the needs of others. After all, we are in the era of modern technology which can assist us with mapping strategies, teleconferencing, and cell phones to contact each other.

A Time of Harvest

We can use technologies to keep in contact so that we are not alienated from the elderly or the youth so that we influence the young with our walk of faith, and so that we draw with lovingkindness. Finally, it is through our outreach efforts that we will receive some of our rewards in Heaven.

Impersonal methods of reaching out just don't touch others like one-on-one testimonies. Ministering the Word of God through tracts, love baskets, and home visits (if welcomed) are more relationship-oriented ways to reach people. Hospital, nursing home, and prison ministries are good training grounds for your ministry associates as well as to those being developed. Youth and young adults can even be trained in ventures to assist the homeless such as outdoor camps where homeless people can come and receive emergency hygiene packages, take a shower, receive food, water, and clean essentials. Community Gardens can be started to help the community, the homeless, and our youth by giving them the chance to fellowship with others and by learning a trade as gardeners. We have to work together for the good of the community. For example, if four churches pooled their resources, they could easily staff a small tent city. Could outdoor showers be installed? Perhaps we should invest in projects of this nature rather than the heavy expenses of larger building projects. Tents with showers and cots would work because the cost factors which would be much less and more manageable. Let's utilize our faith and ask God to provide these resources.

Bottom Line:

We must sacrifice more time to spreading the Word of God through love and deeds, have more accountability, and do more work for the Kingdom. We must also teach others to avoid sin and to confess and repent whether sins are committed on purpose (sins of commission) or by failing to do what should be done (sins of omission). Just as Jesus became the example, we are to show love towards people from the heart, especially those who are lost ... *Lest We Ourselves Stumble.*

> *But he that knew not, and did commit things worthy of stripes, shall be beaten with few stripes. For unto whomsoever much is given, of him shall be much required: and to whom men have committed much, of him they will ask the more.*
> Luke 12:48

A Time of Miracles

Let us consider the greatness of God's manifested power when we operate together in the spirit of unity. When the operation of the gifts, talents, and resources are exercised together for the common good of Gods glory, we see the manifestation of miracles in the lives of sinners. It is then when we are truly operating in the spirit of unity.

> *And he gave some, apostles; and some, prophets; and some, evangelists; and some, pastors and teachers; For the perfecting of the saints, for the work of the ministry, for the edifying of the body of Christ: Till we all come in the unity of the faith,*

*and of the knowledge of the Son of God, unto a perfect man,
unto the measure of the stature of the fulness of Christ:
That we henceforth be no more children, tossed to and fro,
and carried about with every wind of doctrine, by the sleight
of men, and cunning craftiness, whereby they lie in wait to
deceive; But speaking the truth in love, may grow up into him
in all things, which is the head, even Christ: From whom the
whole body fitly joined together and compacted by that which
every joint supplieth, according to the effectual working in
the measure of every part, maketh increase of the body
unto the edifying of itself in love.*
Ephesians 4:11-16

The gifts are given for wise operation, to edify the church, build up the Saints, and build the Kingdom to do the work. When it gleans to us, it is the Kingdom of God, not a building made by hands, not a particular religion or a practiced activity, operating in the purpose God designed to build the Kingdom of God and to perfect the Saints for the ministry. The church, despite the challenges and complexities, will remain a place of miracles. So, as leaders, *We Will Not Stumble*.

A Place of Joy

*His lord said unto him, Well done, good and faithful servant;
thou hast been faithful over a few things, I will make thee
ruler over many things: enter thou into the joy of thy lord.*
Matthew 25:23

You have not stumbled!

ABOUT THE AUTHOR

Kim Austin is married to Johnnie Austin, who assists her with the ministry. They have three adult children and currently reside in Mercer, Tennessee. A native of Detroit, Michigan, Kim ministers wherever she goes. Former Law Enforcement Executive, Criminal Justice Instructor, and now Civil and Family Mediator, she has listened to many people who were disheartened with the local church assembly. As a servant of God, she has encouraged many to seek salvation, live the Word of God, and assist with Kingdom Building. Kim has always been in the helping professions. She is a graduate of the Tennessee School of Religion.

Kim has served and been taught and trained by many great men and women of God. She serves in the gifted area of Prophetess, currently faithfully serveing under Bishop Connie Wright at The House of Faith Ministries and serves in the Intercessory Prayer and Jail Ministries. She received Christ at twelve years old. She served and was trained at Tennessee Baptist MBC under the late Harry Napoleon; Jamison Temple MBC under Pastors Homer and Royal Jamison. She also was trained by the late Bishop Jesse T. Stacks, Mother Gertrude Stacks, the late Mother Estella Boyd of Shalom Temple, and Pastor Edwin Ross of Praying Church Ministries, all in Detroit, Michigan.

In Tennessee, she served as Associate Minister for five years at Bethlehem MBC under Pastor David L. Perry. She also has worked with the Bethlehem MBC, Judgement House Ministry. She shares the Word of God wherever she goes; Kim loves God and loves God's people.

Note from the Publisher

Are you a first time author?

Not sure how to proceed to get your book published?
Want to keep all your rights and all your royalties?
Want it to look as good as a Top 10 publisher?
Need help with editing, layout, cover design?
Want it out there selling in 90 days or less?

Visit our website for some exciting new options!

www.chalfant-eckert-publishing.com

www.ingramcontent.com/pod-product-compliance
Lightning Source LLC
Chambersburg PA
CBHW071814090426
42737CB00012B/2075